DATE DUE

JOHANNES SCOTUS ERIGENA
A STUDY IN MEDIAEVAL PHILOSOPHY

JOHANNES SCOTUS ERIGENA

A STUDY IN MEDIAEVAL PHILOSOPHY

BY

HENRY BETT, M.A.

NEW YORK

RUSSELL & RUSSELL · INC

1964

TO

WILBERT FRANCIS HOWARD

FIRST PUBLISHED IN 1925
REISSUED, 1964, BY RUSSELL & RUSSELL, INC.
BY ARRANGEMENT WITH CAMBRIDGE UNIVERSITY PRESS
L. C. CATALOG CARD NO: 64—10382

PRINTED IN THE UNITED STATES OF AMERICA

PREFACE

IT is rather a reproach to English philosophical literature that there has not existed in our language hitherto anything like a complete treatise on Erigena. There have only been some brief studies, excellent in their way, but not professing to give a full exposition of the Scot's doctrine.

I feel therefore that this volume may reasonably claim to fill a real gap, but no one can be more conscious than I am of the deficiencies both of the book and of the writer.

I should like to acknowledge thankfully much kind encouragement from Professor T. F. Tout, Professor Samuel Alexander, and the Rev. Dr S. H. Mellone, of Manchester; Professor A. E. Taylor, of Edinburgh; and Professor Clement C. J. Webb, of Oxford; and some helpful suggestions from my colleague, the Rev. Dr Frederic Platt. I would also make grateful mention of the unfailing courtesy and help of the officials of the Reading Room at the British Museum, and of the Rylands Library and the University Library at Manchester.

The numbers which are quoted in the text refer to the columns in the edition of Erigena's writings by H. J. Floss, in the *Patrologia Latina* of the Abbé Migne, Vol. 122.

H. B.

February, 1925.

CONTENTS

I. THE LIFE AND WRITINGS OF ERIGENA

JOHANNES SCOTUS ERIGENA is the loneliest figure in the history of European thought. He lived in the ninth century, a dreary epoch, but he was less a man of his generation than any personage whose lot was cast in the Middle Ages, with the possible exception of Frederick of Sicily, and the king, like the philosopher, was born out of due time. Erigena derived all his intellectual inspiration from writers who lived several centuries before him; he made comparatively little impression, by his own writings, upon the thought of his own generation; and whatever adequate appreciation of his remarkable genius there has ever been belongs to modern times. To find such a thinker in such an age (as has been finely said) is like encountering a supreme monument of art in the midst of the sandy wastes of the desert[1].

The whole setting of his life is paradoxical. At a period when the Eastern and the Western Churches were drifting further than ever apart Erigena was the one great thinker alive in the West, and all his sympathies were with the

[1] Il est fort curieux de voir, au milieu de cette ignorance générale, à une époque où la sphère des études était si étroite, un homme, un seul homme, s'élancer dans la plus haute région des spéculations abstraites : il est curieux de voir la philosophie du moyen âge débuter par une entreprise aussi hardie et par un ordre de conceptions aussi singulier. Jean Scot montre par son style qu'il n'était pas étranger à l'étude des bons modèles ; il ose penser d'après lui-même ; il ne manque ni d'une certaine élévation dans les idées, ni d'une certaine méthode dans la manière de les déduire. L'apparition d'un tel homme, à une telle époque, est à tous égards un phénomène extraordinaire : on croit rencontrer un monument de l'art debout au milieu des sables du désert. Degérando, *Histoire comparée des Systèmes de Philosophie*, IV. p. 353.

East. The range of his studies and speculations might have fitted him for the period of the Renaissance, but they made him almost incomprehensible to his own generation, which was more intellectually cramped than perhaps any period in European history before or since. All his intellectual affinities were with the Neoplatonists, almost a thousand years before, and with the modern idealists, almost a thousand years after.

John the Scot was an Irishman. It is expressly stated by Prudentius of Troyes, who had been his friend in early life, that he came from Hibernia[1]. He was known, in his lifetime, as Joannes Scotus, Scottus, or Scotigena[2]. Prudentius of Troyes, Pardulus of Laon, and the canons of the Synods of Valence and Langres refer to him as Scotus. Hincmar and the papal librarian, Anastasius, use the form Scotigena. In the oldest manuscripts of his translation of the pseudo-Dionysius (and there only) he is designated Joannes Jerugena. It is probable that he had formed this cognomen on the model of Grajugena, his own name for Maximus, in the verses that he wrote upon the *Ambigua*[3]. While Jerugena is the oldest form that appears in the manuscripts, Erugena and Eriugena speedily appear. Erigena is not found until later[4]. The name is probably formed from the

---

[1] *Te solum acutissimum Galliae transmisit Hibernia. De Praedestinatione contra Joannem Scotum*, c. xiv (Migne, *Patrol. Lat.* Vol. 115, 1194 A).

[2] Ireland was known as *Scotia major*. Bede, in his enthusiastic description of Ireland, writes (*Hist. Eccles.* I. i) *Haec autem proprie patria Scottorum est, ab hac egressi, ut diximus, tertiam in Britannia Britonibus et Pictis gentem addiderunt.*

[3] Floss, 1236.

> Quisquis amat formam pulchrae laudare Sophiae,
> Te legat assiduo, Maxime Grajugena.

[4] R. L. Poole, *Illustrations of the History of Medieval Thought*, pp. 55–56. Mr R. L. Poole concludes that it is "an unwelcome consequence" of the fact

Greek 'Ιέρνη or the Celtic Ériu, Érinn[1], and possibly modified to suggest ἱερός—ἱεροῦ (νήσου), *ex insula sanctorum*, since
Ireland already had that character[2]. Erigena's Irish origin is
strongly supported by the fact that he was distinguished for
his knowledge of Greek, as the monasteries of Ireland were
almost the only places in Europe where the study of Greek
survived in those dark and turbulent days[3].

Erigena's birth must be dated within the early years of
the ninth century, about 800–815. He went abroad, and
was at the court of Charles the Bald, some time before 847,
for by that year Prudentius had left the court to become
Bishop of Troyes, and he mentions his former friendship
with Erigena there[4]. The philosopher's life seems to have
been unsettled and unfortunate up to this time, and he found
at Charles' court a haven of security[5]. The king is said

that Scotigena and Jerugena are now shown to be the earlier forms of our
philosopher's name, "that the time-honoured title of Erigena must be finally
withdrawn from currency" (p. 56). But general usage and general convenience
must surely overrule a pedantic accuracy. "John the Scot" is an awkward
title when in constant use; moreover, there were others of the name; and it
has never been seriously proposed to revive "Scotigena" or "Jerugena." The
prescription of ten centuries is warrant enough for us still to call the philosopher
"Erigena."

[1] Sir John Rhys, *Celtic Britain*, p. 266.

[2] Floss, *Prooem.* XX. Christlieb, *Leben u. Lehre d. Johannes Scotus Erigena*,
p. 16. This involves a grammatical solecism, for νῆσος is feminine. See Huber,
Johannes Scotus Erigena, p. 39. The conjecture of Gale, that John's birthplace
was a place once called Eriuven in Herefordshire, and that of Dempster, that
it was Ayr in Scotland, are not worth discussing. There is not a shadow of
evidence or likelihood for either.

[3] A la fin du sixième siècle, il n'y a plus, des rives du Rhin aux gorges des
Pyrénées, un coin si retiré où n'ait pénétré le fléau de la barbarie. L'Irlande
seule, défendue par une double mer, n'a pas encore subi l'invasion étrangère.
Hauréau, *Singularités Historiques et Littéraires*, p. 4. See also Neander,
History of the Church, VI. p. 161.

[4] *Quo te familiarius amplectebar peculiarius diligebam.* Prudentius, *De Praed.*
c. i.   [5] *De Praed.* (*Praefatio*) 355 B.

to have made the Scot head of the palace school (*schola palatina*)[1]. The school of the palace dated from the days of Charlemagne and Alcuin, and had been, at first, something between a seminary for the young princes, and an academy for the entourage of the Emperor. The "palatine erudition" was famous for a couple of generations after the death of Charlemagne[2].

Charles the Bald and the philosopher seem to have been on most intimate terms. There is a tradition that John was once dining with the King, who, provoked by some offence against Gallic manners on the part of the philosopher, asked him: *Quid distat inter Scottum et sottum?* John retorted across the board: *Tabula tantum*[3]! Erigena's own references to the King, in his extant poems and dedications, sufficiently witness to the regard that existed between them[4].

The little town of Paris was not yet as important as it was destined to become, but it was a favourite residence of the King, and it owed much of its increasing prominence to the neighbourhood of the Abbey of St Denys, which had become the burial-place of the dynasty[5]. It was believed that the monastery had been founded by Dionysius the Areopagite, the convert of the Apostle Paul at Athens. This identification of Denys, the apostle of Gaul, with Dionysius was universally accepted at the time and indeed was not seriously doubted until it was challenged by Abailard, three hundred years later. The traditional belief was that the Areopagite had been converted to the Christian faith when the Apostle

[1] Montalembert, *Monks of the West*, II. p. 227.

[2] Guizot, *History of Civilisation in France*, II. pp. 238–243.

[3] William of Malmesbury, *De Pontif. Angl.* V.

[4] See the Scot's poems, especially *Carm.* I. 2, 3, 4, and V. 20 (1240)—a Greek poem.

[5] R. L. Poole, *Illustrations of the History of Medieval Thought*, p. 57.

was telling the story of the Passion, and the supernatural darkness which accompanied it. This darkness had greatly impressed Dionysius, who had been at Heliopolis on the day of the Crucifixion, and had exclaimed at the time: "Either the Divinity suffers, or sympathises with the sufferer[1]!" The Apostle Paul made Dionysius the Bishop of Athens. Later in life he journeyed into Gaul, and was martyred[2] at Paris with Rusticus and Eleutherius, his two companions[3].

The works which he was believed to have written, on *The Divine Names*, *The Mystic Theology*, *The Heavenly Hierarchy*, and *The Ecclesiastical Hierarchy*, with some *Epistles*, really date, in all probability, from early in the sixth century[4], and are the production of some Syrian monk who wrote under Monophysite influences. The writings are deeply impregnated with the later Neoplatonism. The whole style of thought and language, the formal use of Scripture, the quotation of a famous passage from Ignatius[5], and an allusion to "the philosopher Clement[6]," all unite to make it fantastically impossible that the Areopagite should have written these treatises. Moreover, the earliest quotations from the Dionysian writings are found in the works of Severus, the Monophysite patriarch of Antioch, about 512–

---

[1] ἢ τὸ θεῖον πάσχει, ἢ τῷ πάσχοντι συμπάσχει. Suidas (*in Dionysio*). But see Dionysius, *Epp.* IV. and XI.

[2] *Breviarium Romanum*, Oct. 9.

[3] The legend in the Breviary is that after he was beheaded he walked two miles carrying his severed head in his hand. Someone once asked Ninon de l'Enclos if she believed that St Denys had walked *all* that way with his burden. "Pourquoi pas, Mademoiselle?" said Ninon, "ce n'est que le premier pas qui coûte!"

[4] See Westcott's *Religious Thought in the West*, pp. 152, 153.

[5] *De Div. Nom.* IV. 12, ὁ ἐμὸς ἔρως ἐσταύρωται. *Ep. ad Romanos*, VII. 2.

[6] *De Div. Nom.* V. 9.

518, and of Andrew, the Archbishop of Caesarea in Cappadocia, probably about 520[1]. Again, Dionysius is acquainted with the liturgical custom of singing the *Credo* during the Mass[2], which was introduced by the Monophysites at Antioch in 471 and soon afterward adopted by the Catholics.

But the late origin of these writings was utterly unsuspected in the ninth century, and the growing fame of the Abbey of St Denys naturally induced lively interest in the supposed writings of its supposed founder. Copies were kept in the Abbey which had been sent to Pippin by Pope Paul the First, in 757, to the Abbot Fuldrad by Pope Hadrian the First, a few years later, and to Lewis the Pious by the Byzantine Emperor Michael the Stammerer, in 827[3]. Hildwin, the Abbot of St Denys, had made an abortive attempt to translate them. Charles the Bald gave the task of translation into the more capable hands of Erigena, apparently before he had been long in France[4], and this became a determining experience of the philosopher's life.

Erigena also translated the *Ambigua* of Maximus the Confessor, and his own thought was somewhat influenced by the treatise. Maximus (580–662) had been the secretary of the Emperor Heraclius. He became a monk, and finally Abbot of his monastery at Chrysopolis near Constantinople. He was a leading controversialist against the Monothelites[5].

---

[1] Bardenhewer, *Patrology*, pp. 539, 540.
[2] *De eccl. Hier.* III. 2. Duchesne, *Les Origines du Culte Chrétien*, p. 84.
[3] Christlieb, *Leben u. Lehre d. Johannes Scotus Erigena*, p. 26. R. L. Poole, *Illustrations of the History of Medieval Thought*, p. 57.
[4] See the poem prefixed to the version of Dionysius.
[5] Mr R. L. Poole, in *Illustrations of the History of Medieval Thought* (p. 58), refers to "the *monothelite* monk Maximus." This is a slip. Maximus was fiercely duothelite. "Der zuvor genannte Mönch Maximus ist derselbe, welcher im Monotheletenstreit der eifrigste Verfechter der Lehre von einem

He travelled in Egypt, and in 645 went to Rome, where he was on intimate terms with Pope Martin the First. In 653 the Emperor Constans the Second, who favoured the Monothelite heresy, had him arrested, tried for sedition and banished to Thrace. His largest work is a commentary on the obscure passages of Dionysius and Gregory Nazianzen. This is the *Ambigua*, which Erigena translated. His version, or rather all of it that is extant, is only about one-seventh of the whole work[1].

Erigena was involved in two theological controversies of the period. One was the dispute about Predestination that arose out of the writings of Gottschalk. Hincmar, the Archbishop of Rheims, requested the Scot to reply to the Saxon monk. He consented, and issued his tract, *On Predestination*, in 851. It proved a most embarrassing defence, for the Scot advanced his favourite doctrine that evil has no real being, and thus dissolved the usual elements of the controversy[2]. The essence of God is single, he argues, but our minds are compelled to regard it under manifold aspects. Thus we distinguish the will of God from the love of God, and from the wisdom of God. But these are merely thoughts by which our human minds symbolise to themselves the nature of God, which is essential unity. Therefore the Divine Predestination is simply one amongst many of our subjective conceptions of God. Moreover, it cannot be that God should

doppelten Willen Christi war." Baur, *Lehre v. d. Dreieinigkeit*, II. p. 264. See also Mosheim, *Ecclesiastical History*, II. ii. 2.

[1] That Erigena did actually translate the whole of the *Ambigua* appears from the fact that the fragment published under the title *De egressu et regressu animae ad Deum* (in Floss, 1023) is really the last page but one of his version of the *Ambigua*, corresponding with the passage in Maximus, 1416 A.D. (Vol. 91, ed. Migne).

[2] *Peccatum, mors, miseria, a Deo non sunt. Eorum igitur causa Deus non est. De Praed.* 366 B. This is the real thesis of the treatise.

will anything but what is essentially good, and essentially real, since He is the supreme good and the supreme reality. But sin and misery and death are the negation of being and the negation of good. Therefore God cannot in any sense will the misery of men, either here or hereafter, nor the death of the soul. Sin and all its consequences must be regarded as a lapse from reality, as well as a lapse from good, on the part of the created will. The eternal fire is metaphorical. The righteous will delight in the same element, so to speak, as that in which the wicked will suffer, as light delights the healthy eye and pains the eye that is diseased—a favourite image, borrowed from Augustine[1], which reappears numberless times in Erigena's writings.

Gottschalk's doctrine of Predestination (which Erigena calls, in phrases that would have delighted John Wesley, *monstrosum, venenosum, mortiferum dogma*, and *stultissima, crudelissimaque insania*)[2] is thus disposed of effectively enough from the philosopher's point of view, but it is not surprising that the ecclesiastics of the ninth century were horrified quite as much by Erigena's unique defence of orthodoxy as they had been by Gottschalk's heresy.

Erigena's views were condemned a few years later at the Synod of Valence, in 855, where his doctrines were unkindly described, in the sixth canon, as "Scots' porridge," *pultes Scotorum*[3]. Four years later they were condemned again at the Synod of Langres.

Erigena also took part in the Eucharistic controversy of the century, started by Paschasius Radbertus in 831. The

[1] *Conf.* VII. 16. *De Civ. Dei*, XXII. 2.
[2] *De Praed.* 360 A and *Epilog.* 438 D.
[3] The insulting phrase was not original, for Jerome once described Coelestius, the friend and follower of Pelagius, as "stodged with Scots' porridge" (*Scotorum pultibus praegravatus*).

Scot's work on the subject is lost. That which was condemned by the Council of Vercelli in 1050, and long attributed to Erigena, is almost certainly by Ratramnus of Corvey[1]. It is not wonderful that it should have been ascribed to Erigena in an uncritical age, for the book takes a surprisingly liberal and rational view of the Eucharist[2], very much along the line of Erigena's own doctrine. We know the Scot's position in the dispute from what is said by his adversaries, and also from what he himself says elsewhere. Hincmar, for example, condemns as one of the opinions of Erigena the doctrine that the Eucharist is *non verum corpus et verus sanguis Domini, sed tantum memoria veri corporis et sanguinis Ejus*[3]. Erigena himself, in his *Exposition of the Heavenly Hierarchy* of the pseudo-Dionysius, describes the Eucharist as *typicam similitudinem spiritualis participationis Jesu, quam fideliter solo intellectu gustamus*[4]. And in his *Commentary on St John's Gospel*, he writes *Nam et nos, qui post peractam ejus incarnationem et passionem et resurrectionem in eum credimus, ejusque mysteria,*

---

[1] R. L. Poole, *Illustrations of the History of Medieval Thought*, p. 59 *n*.

[2] The treatise *De Corpore et Sanguine Domini* is reprinted in Migne (*Patrol. Lat.* Vol. 121). Two passages which occur toward the end of the work will sufficiently illustrate the doctrine of Ratramnus: *Docemur a salvatore, necnon a sancto Paulo apostolo, quod iste panis et iste calix qui super altare ponitur, in figuram sive in memoriam Dominicae mortis ponantur, et quod gestum est in praeterito, praesenti revocet memoriae, ut illius passionis memores effecti....Nec ideo quoniam ista dicimus, putetur in mysterio sacramenti corpus Domini, vel sanguinem ipsius, non a fidelibus sumi, quando fides, non quod oculus videt, sed quod credit, accipit; quoniam spiritualis est esca, et spiritualis potus, spiritualiter animam pascens, et aeternae satietatis vitam tribuens.* It is interesting to note that the Anglican doctrine of the Eucharist is largely derived from this treatise of Ratramnus. Cranmer and Ridley studied it together. See R. D. Hampden, *The Scholastic Philosophy*, pp. 320, 527, and Browne, *Exposition of the Thirty-Nine Articles*, pp. 116, 704.

[3] *De Praed.* c. xxxi.

[4] Floss, 41 C.

quaptum nobis conceditur, intelligimus, et spiritualiter eum immolamus et intellectualiter mente, non dente, comedimus[1].

It has been doubted whether the Scot ever wrote a treatise on the Eucharist at all, but the reference of Hincmar, the existence of the contemporary work of Adrevalt, *De Corpore et Sanguine Christi, contra ineptias Scoti*, the condemnation of a book by Erigena at the Council of Vercelli, the allusion by Lanfranc to a book by Erigena, *De Eucharistia*[2], and the fact that Berengar claimed to be (and was universally regarded as) a follower of Erigena in his Sacramentarian views[3], seem to be conclusive upon the point. The difference in the Latin style, however, is alone sufficient to make it absolutely certain to a modern reader that the treatise *De Corpore et Sanguine Domini* is not the book that was written by Erigena.

[1] *Comment. in Ev. sec. Joan.* 311 B. It looks as if the recantation which Berengar had to sign at the Council of Rome in 1059 was framed expressly in view of this passage. *Panem et vinum, quae in altari ponuntur, post consecrationem non solum sacramentum sed etiam verum corpus et sanguinem Domini nostri esse; et sensualiter non solum sacramento, sed in veritate manibus sacerdotum tractari; et frangi et fidelium dentibus atteri.*

[2] Christlieb, *Leben u. Lehre d. Johannes Scotus Erigena*, p. 78.

[3] Berengar wrote to Lanfranc, at that time prior of Bec in Normandy: *Pervenit ad me, frater Lanfranc, quiddam auditum ab Ingelranno Carnotensi, in quo dissimulare non debui ammonere dilectionem tuam. Id autem est, displicere tibi, immo haereticas habuisse sententias Joannis Scoti de Sacramento altaris, in quibus dissentit a suscepto tuo Paschasio....Si haereticum habes Joannem, cujus sententias de Eucharistia probamus; habendus tibi est haereticus Ambrosius, Hieronymus, Augustinus, ut de caeteris taceam.* See Gieseler, *Ecclesiastical History*, II. p. 399, and Neander, *History of the Church*, VI. p. 227. Berengar's reference to the Scot's doctrine as being that the consecrated elements are *figuram, signum, pignus corporis et sanguinis Domini* (Floss, *Prooem.* XXI.) certainly looks as if he were quoting from the treatise of Ratramnus (where these terms perpetually recur) and attributing it to Erigena. But even this is evidence that the Scot did write upon the Eucharist. As Mr R. L. Poole has said: "It was known that he had written a treatise, and therefore the only appropriate treatise that came to hand was fathered upon him." (*Illustrations of the History of Medieval Thought*, p. 59 *n.*)

The authenticity of some of the smaller works attributed to Erigena has been disproved by recent criticism. *The Exposition of the Mystical Theology* of Dionysius is certainly not Erigena's, for the commentary is based upon the Latin translation of Johannes Saracenus, which dates from the twelfth century. Apparently Erigena did not write any *Exposition of the Ecclesiastical Hierarchy* of Dionysius, for what is printed under that title by Migne consists of four fragments from Erigena's preface to his version of Dionysius, and from his rendering of the *Ecclesiastical Hierarchy*, with another fragment of Hildwin's *Areopagitica* sandwiched between. Another fragment which Migne prints under the title *De egressu et regressu animae ad Deum* is only a part of Erigena's version of the *Ambigua* of Maximus[1].

Since Floss' edition of the writings of Erigena was published, two other treatises have come to light which are probably the work of the Scot. One is a short life of Boethius, contained in an eleventh century manuscript, written in an Irish hand, and expressly describing itself as *verba Johannis Scoti*. The other is a set of glosses on Martianus Capella, discovered by Hauréau, and believed by him to be the work of Erigena[2].

Sometime about 860, Pope Nicholas the First wrote to Charles the Bald demanding that Erigena's version of Dionysius should be sent to him for examination[3]. It is needless to observe that there was no suspicion attaching to

---

[1] Compare, in Migne's edition of Erigena, 265 D–267 A, 268 C, with 1033 C–1034 C, 1069 D–1072 A. Also compare 267 B–268 A with Hildwin's *Areopagitica* (30 A, C, Vol. 106, ed. Migne). See Draeseke (and Brilliantoff) in *Zeitschrift für wissenschaftliche Theologie*, 47 (1904).

[2] M. Hauréau printed some specimens of the commentary on Martianus Capella in *Notices et Extraits*, XX. 2.

[3] R. L. Poole, *Illustrations of the History of Medieval Thought*, p. 58.

the writings of Dionysius. It was the translator who was suspect, on account of his rumoured opinions, *qui non sane sapere in quibusdam frequenti rumore dicatur*, as the Pope's letter has it. There was his tract on Predestination, which had been in existence now for nine or ten years. And there was graver matter still, in view of the widening breach between the Eastern and the Western Church, in the Scot's admiration for Greek writers. Worst of all—if these were known at the time—were his mediating doctrine as to the Procession of the Holy Spirit, and his daring verses exalting Constantinople above Rome.

> *Constantinopolis florens nova Roma vocatur,*
> *Moribus et muris Roma vetusta cadis.*
> *Transiit imperium, mansitque superbia tecum,*
> *Cultus avaritiae te nimium superat*[1].

The King seems to have taken no notice of the Pope's summons, but there can be little doubt that the philosopher must have felt himself generally suspected as a heretic in these years.

It is impossible to fix with any precision the date of Erigena's greatest work, which characteristically bears a Greek title, περὶ φύσεως μερισμοῦ, *id est, de Divisione Naturae*. It must have been written later than the translations of Dionysius and Maximus, and the treatise on Predestination, for much of its teaching is a derivation from the former, and a development of the latter. It seems probable that it appeared before the death of Charles the Bald, and during Erigena's residence in France. We may guess that the work probably dates from 865–870. It consists of five books, and runs to nearly six hundred closely printed columns in the edition of Migne[2]. It is almost equal in bulk to all the

---

[1] Floss, 1194 B.

[2] Thomas Gale, who was Professor of Greek at Cambridge (1666), and

rest of the Scot's writings put together, including the translations.

The end of Erigena's life is involved in much obscurity. It is inferred, from a poem that he wrote commemorating the foundation of a church, believed to be that at Compiègne, which Charles began in the year of his death, that John was in France in 877[1]. The following year Alfred defeated the Danes at the great battle of Ethandun, and there was peace in England, after many years of war. This fact, along with the death of Erigena's patron, Charles the Bald, lends an initial probability to the story told by William of Malmesbury[2] that the Scot came to England, on the invitation of Alfred, and taught at the Abbey of Malmesbury, where, some years afterward, his scholars stabbed him to death with their pens, *a pueris quos docebat, graphiis perfossus.*

afterwards Headmaster of St Paul's (1672), and Dean of York (1697), issued the first printed edition of the *De Divisione Naturae* at Oxford in 1681. The volume contained also the Scot's version of the *Ambigua* of Maximus. Dr C. B. Schlüter, a Professor at Münster in Westphalia, published an edition of the *De Divisione Naturae*, along with Erigena's poems, in 1838. The best edition is that of H. J. Floss, in the *Patrologia Latina* of the Abbé Migne (Vol. 122), which contains the whole of Erigena's writings. It is far from perfect, however. The best MSS were not used by Floss, and presumably were not known to him. "Zu den von Floss in der Ausgabe (Migne 122, 411–1022) benutzten Hss. Sangerm. 309. s. xi, 280. s. xii, 830. s. xi. und Paris 1764. s. xii. kommen noch Bamberg H. J. iv. 5 und 6 sowie Avranches 230 (vgl. A. Schmitt, *Zwei noch unbenutzte Hss. des Joh. Scotus Erigena*, Bamberg, 1900) sowie Cantabrig. Trin. Coll. O. 5. 20. s. xii. Für die Herstellung des Textes aber sind besonders wichtig Rem. 875 und Bamberg H. J. iv. 5 und 6, da beide Hss. in Reims geschrieben und mit Noten von Johannes' eigener Hand verstehen sind; die Noten der Bamberger Hss. aber sind im Paris 12964. s. xi. schon verarbeitet; so gehen wenigstens zwei Hss. auf Johannes' eigene Zeit zurück" (Manitius, *Geschichte d. lat. Literatur d. Mittelalters*, p. 335). A really critical edition of the writings of Erigena is much to be desired.

[1] R. L. Poole, *Illustrations of the History of Medieval Thought*, p. 59 *n.*

[2] He tells the story thrice, in substantially the same terms, in the *Gesta Regum*, the *Gesta Pontificum*, and in the *Epistle to Peter.*

Apart from the bizarre climax, there is nothing unlikely in this. There is no doubt at all as to the person the chronicler intends to describe, for he knows of Erigena's presence at the court of Charles the Bald, of his translation of the works of Dionysius[1], and of his own great work, which is cited by its Greek title, *Periphysion*, with the appropriate comment that it is "extremely useful in solving the perplexity of certain indispensable enquiries, if he be pardoned for some things in which he deviated from the opinions of the Latins through too close attention to the Greeks."

The monastic chronicler goes on to say that John's body lay for a time in the church of St Lawrence, but a heavenly light appearing there night by night admonished the monks to bury the dead sophist in the Abbey Church (*in majorem ecclesiam*) on the left of the altar, where this inscription was placed upon his tomb[2]:

> *Conditus hoc tumulo, sanctus sophista Joannes*[3],
> *Qui ditatus erat vivens iam dogmate miro,*
> *Martyrio tandem meruit conscendere coelum,*
> *Quo semper regnant cuncti per secula sancti*[4].

[1] The fact that John the Scot had translated the writings of Dionysius seems to have been quite familiarly known in England in the Middle Ages. John of Trevisa (1326–1412) mentions it casually in one of his prefaces, the *Dialogue between a Lord and a Clerk* (quoted in G. G. Coulton's *Social Life in England from the Conquest to the Reformation*, p. 179), "Also, at prayenge of kyng Charles, Johan Scot translated Denys bokes out of greke in to latyn, and then out of latyn in to frensshe; then what hath Englysshe trespaced that it might not be translated in to Englysshe?"

[2] The monument of which William of Malmesbury speaks was removed along with other monuments, toward the end of the eleventh century, by the command of Abbot Warin, and stowed away in a corner of St Michael's Church. Leland states, in his *Itinerary*, that the statue in the Abbey Church bore the inscription *Joannes Scotus qui transtulit Dionysium e Greco in Latinum.*

[3] He was called by his contemporaries *Joannes Sophista* and *Joannes Sapiens.*

[4] R. L. Poole, *Illustrations of the History of Medieval Thought*, p. 320. Huber, *Johannes Scotus Erigena*, p. 112.

This straightforward story would probably have carried conviction still, as it did in the Middle Ages, but for the circumstance that it has been discredited and confused through the introduction, by modern biographers of Erigena, of three other passages from mediaeval chronicles.

The Chronicle of Asser mentions a certain Grimbald, priest and monk, and a certain John, priest and monk, who came from Gaul at the invitation of King Alfred. Later on, in another section of his history, Asser relates Alfred's foundation of the monastery of Athelney, describes its first Abbot as John, the Old-Saxon, and narrates the attempt by the servants of two Gaulish monks in the house to murder him by night in the church. Then the spurious Chronicle of Ingulf of Croyland has confused John the Old-Saxon, whom the writer knew of from Asser, with Erigena, of whom he had read in William of Malmesbury, and this has misled almost every succeeding writer.

There is no reason why William of Malmesbury's story should not be accepted as substantially true. The citation by the Pope, the condemnation by the Synods, the death of his friend Wulfad (who might otherwise have been a protector, since he was Archbishop of Bourges) in 876, and the death of Charles the Bald, a year later, all make Erigena's retreat into England look likely. Moreover, Malmesbury had been founded by an Irish monk, Maeldun, and had a definite tradition of Irish culture[1]. On this account it was probably the one monastery in England to which an Irish scholar coming from the Continent would be most likely to resort—a significant fact which seems to have escaped all

[1] Zimmer, *The Irish Element in Mediaeval Culture*, p. 37. Dugdale, *Monasticon Anglicanum*, I. p. 253. There are distinct traces of Irish artistic influence in the architecture of several churches in the neighbourhood of Malmesbury.

those who have previously written of Erigena's life. It is
difficult to believe that William of Malmesbury, a particularly honest and painstaking chronicler, could be altogether
wrong in a story which was a tradition of his own monastery,
and which he tells with such accuracy of circumstantial
detail. Asser's first allusion to John the priest and monk,
the companion of Grimbald, may possibly refer to John the
Scot, but his later mention of John the Old-Saxon, who
became the first Abbot of Athelney, manifestly refers to
another person. The forger of the Chronicle of Ingulf merely
confuses John the Scot, as described by William of Malmesbury, with Asser's John the Old-Saxon[1]. In later days the
matter was further complicated by the fact that the description of John the Scot in his epitaph as a martyr led to his
being confused with John Scot, Bishop of Mecklenburg, who
was slain on the 10th of November, 1066, and was afterwards
commemorated as a martyr on that date[2]. After 1586 the
name was omitted from the martyrologies, probably on
account of this confusion.

There is a comparatively modern legend that Erigena
travelled in Greece and there found a lost treatise of Aristotle,
by enquiry of an oracle. This rests upon a mere confusion
of names. The story is told of himself by John, the son of
Patricius, who was a Spaniard, and who translated the
Secreta Secretorum, attributed in the Middle Ages to Aristotle. The confusion dates from the sixteenth century[3], and
has been perpetuated by almost every subsequent writer

---

[1] Most of the authorities, including Hauréau and Huber, are hopelessly
confused, mainly because they regarded Ingulf as a genuine authority. All the
facts are disentangled in a masterly manner by Mr R. L. Poole, *Illustrations of
the History of Medieval Thought*, pp. 313-329.

[2] R. L. Poole, *Illustrations of the History of Medieval Thought*, p. 327.

[3] Bale, *Script. ill. Britann.* II. 24, p. 124, and Aubrey, *Miscellanies*, p. 168.

who has touched upon Erigena's life, until the false attri-
bution was exposed in our own days[1] by one of the most
acute and learned of English scholars, who has done more
than anyone else to elucidate the facts of Erigena's life.

Erigena wrote Latin in a clear and correct style. In
Greek his scholarship was more moderate, though sufficient
to astonish his age. In his preface to his translation of the
writings of the pseudo-Dionysius he confesses himself a
beginner in Greek[2]. The confession is confirmed by the
very literal character of the version and by some obvious
errors. But such Greek scholarship as Erigena had was
altogether remarkable in his generation, for he could read
and render the language with substantial accuracy[3]. In any
case, he must have been, as has been said, "one of the last
in Western Europe to possess an effective knowledge of
Greek before it ceased for six centuries[4]." Anastasius, the
papal librarian, thought it a very miracle that a man of such
learning should be found at the ends of the earth (*in finibus
mundi*)[5].

Erigena never called himself nor was called by his contemporaries an ecclesiastic. In the letter of Pope Nicholas

[1] R. L. Poole, *Illustrations of the History of Medieval Thought*, pp. 311–
312.

[2] ......*rudes admodum tirones adhuc helladicorum studiorum fatemur.* More
than once, in his version of the *Ambigua*, he renders πέδαις by *pueris* (1197 D,
1198 A, D).

[3] Jean Scot sait le grec, et il ne le sait pas comme Béda, comme Alcuin,
comme Heiric, comme Remi d'Auxerre et tant d'autres apprentis hellénistes
de l'école latine, qui, pour avoir quelques mots de grec en commerçant avec
les Irlandais, en font grande parade, et trahissent ensuite par les plus bouffonnes
erreurs l'imperfection de leur savoir. Il sait le grec autant qu'un érudit du
XVIe siècle, et sa traduction des œuvres de faux Denys est aujourd'hui dans
toutes les mains. Hauréau, *Singularités Historiques et Littéraires*, p. 31.

[4] Whittaker, *Apollonius of Tyana and other Essays*, p. 124.

[5] Floss, 1027–1028.

he is referred to as *quidam vir*[1], and Prudentius reproaches him as *barbarum et nullis ecclesiasticae dignitatis gradibus insignitum*[2]. With regard to his person and his temperament he is traditionally described as *perexilis corporis* and *ira praeproperus*[3]. It has been thought that the latter characteristic is corroborated by the violence with which he assails Gottschalk[4]. But considering the controversial methods of those days, that surely goes for very little.

Such are the scanty facts, as far as they are known to us, in the life of John the Scot, the greatest thinker of his own day, and one of the greatest metaphysicians of all time.

[1] Floss, 1025.
[2] *De Praed.* c. iii.
[3] William of Malmesbury, *De Pontif. Angl.* and *Ep. ad Petrum.*
[4] Christlieb, *Leben u. Lehre d. Johannes Scotus Erigena*, p. 58.

II. THE PHILOSOPHY OF ERIGENA: A SUMMARY

THE whole of Erigena's philosophical system is contained in his greatest work, *On the Division of Nature*, as he entitled it. This is in the form of a dialogue between the Master and the Disciple. The dialectical form is of much service and the Disciple is a real participant in the discussion. He is often deliberately led on to draw some startling conclusion, which really is the logical result of the argument, and then the Master proceeds to restate it in a more plausible way, and to defend it from Scripture and the Fathers.

The work is divided into five books, and runs to about a quarter of a million words. The first book deals mainly with the doctrine of God as the source of all; the second with the primal causes, which are a medium between God and the creation; the third with the nature of the created universe; the fourth and the fifth with the return of all to God. There is a good deal of repetition, and each book trespasses considerably upon the special ground of the others, but the five books correspond roughly with Erigena's fourfold division of Nature, the fourth division being regarded as of such importance and of such difficulty that the last two books are devoted to it.

The work is dedicated to Wulfadus, who is described as a beloved brother in Christ, and a companion in studies such as these. Wulfad lived for some time at the court of Charles the Bald, as the tutor of the King's son Carloman. He was a canon of Rheims, and was ordained to the priesthood by Ebbo, Archbishop of that diocese, who was afterwards excommunicated, whereupon those who had been ordained by him were unfrocked. These clerics were reinstated in their orders by Pope Nicholas the First in 865. The next year Wulfad was appointed by the King Archbishop of Bourges. He died ten years later, on the first of April, 876[1].

There is an immense amount of repetition in the work, as has been said, and there are also large tracts of it which consist of nothing but lengthy allegorical expositions of Scripture. All this has been disregarded here[2], and it has been possible, therefore, in the following pages to present a summary of the philosophy of Erigena, almost wholly in his own words, which omits nothing of any real significance, and yet is scarcely one tenth of the bulk of the original.

Occasional passages from Erigena's other writings will be cited in the course of the discussion, but all that is really necessary for the final statement and full understanding of his system may be found in his one great work.

The philosophy of Erigena sets out with several schemes of division which serve as an indispensable basis for all that follows. The supreme division of all things is into things which are (*ea quae sunt*) and things which are not (*ea quae non sunt*). By things which are, we are to understand all that may be comprehended by sense or intellect, and by things which are not, all that surpasses sense and intellect, the very *esse* of which is to lack all comprehensible existence (*essentia*) (643 D). The general name for all things is φύσις, *natura*.

---

[1] Floss, *Prooem.* § 22. Huber, *Johannes Scotus Erigena*, p. 50. Pallet, *Nouvelle Histoire du Berry*, IV. p. 48. *Supplément au Rituel Romain pour le Diocèse de Bourges*, p. 185.

[2] But sufficient illustrations of Erigena's expository methods have been given on pp. 152–7.

The Fourfold Division of Nature. There is a fourfold division of Nature, as (*a*) creating and not created; (*b*) created and creating; (*c*) created and not creating; (*d*) not creating and not created. The germ of this fourfold division is a sentence of Augustine's, "The cause of things, therefore, which makes but is not made, is God; but all other causes both make and are made[1]." The third division is logically opposed to the first, and the fourth to the second. The first and the fourth divisions are to be understood of God, regarded alternately as the source of all, and as the end of all. These divisions are not to be understood as separated in the nature of God: indeed, they are not in God at all, but in our thought of God (526) (1019 A). They are not forms of God, but forms of our thought, because we are compelled, by the very constitution of our minds, to think of a beginning and an end (527). The second and the third divisions, however, do not merely exist in our thought, but in things themselves, in which causes and effects are actually separated (528). The second division represents the primordial causes, of which the Logos is the unity and the aggregate. All that we see divided and multiplex in Nature is one in the primal causes (527 A). The third division represents the created universe; in Erigena's phrase it is all that is known in generation, in time and in space (442).

These divisions of Nature do not mean that God is the genus of the creature, or the creature a species of God, though Gregory Nazianzen does say, *pars Dei sumus*, which is a metaphorical use of language, to express the truth that in God we live and move and have our being (523 D). The four divisions are an example of analysis (ἀναλυτική) descending from the most general to the most special, and

[1] *De Civ. Dei*, v. 9.

then reversing the process, and resolving individuals into species, species into genera, genera into essences, and essences into the wisdom of the Deity (526 A), whence all these divisions arose and where they end.

The Modes of Non-Being. Next in importance to the fourfold division of Nature for the understanding of Erigena's philosophy, is his fivefold division of non-being. It is fundamental to Erigena's scheme that Nature, as the general name for all things, comprises both the things which are and the things which are not. All that is perceived by the senses or understood by the intellect is said to be (*esse*). The five modes of non-being are as follows: 1. All that by reason of the excellence of its nature (*per excellentiam suae naturae*) escapes the reach of the senses and of the intellect. The essence of all things belongs to this category. Whatever is known is a kind of accident of the underlying, unknown and unknowable substance. We know anything by quality and quantity, form, matter, difference, time and space (443 C). But the essence of it, to which these attach themselves, we cannot know. Since this essence cannot be known by us, it does not exist for us. 2. In the order of Nature the affirmation of the higher existence is the denial of the lower, and the denial of the lower existence is the affirmation of the higher. Anything is, in so far as it is known by itself or by what is above it; it is not, in so far as it cannot be comprehended by what is below it (444). 3. All latent or seminal or potential existence. All men who will ever exist were potentially created in the first man; all plants that will ever exist now exist potentially in the seed of existing plants (445 A). But in this sense, actual existence is existence, and potential existence is non-existence. 4. All that exists by generation as a form

of matter in space and time, and is liable to increase and
decrease. All this is not, in the full sense of being. Only
what is solely comprehended by the intellect is real being
(445 C). All else is appearance and not reality. 5. This
last mode of non-being belongs only to human nature. Man
properly is, in so far as he is in the image of God: in so far
as he loses the image of God through sin, he is not. When
it is restored to him in Christ, he is again, as the Apostle
says: *Who calleth the things that are not as though they were*
(Rom. iv. 17) (445 C).

The Affirmative and Negative Theology. Still another
scheme of distinction is important to the understanding of
Erigena's philosophy. He borrowed from the pseudo-
Dionysius the method of the affirmative and negative
theology (*affirmativa et abnegativa*, καταφατική καὶ ἀποφατική) (458 A). Thus the same predicate may rightly be
affirmed and denied of God, but the affirmation is metaphorical (*metaphorice*) and the denial is literal (*proprie*).
This depends upon the fact that every human thought
involves a contrary, and God, as the Absolute, is beyond all
oppositions, for He is the reconciliation of contraries (510 D).
Thus God may be said to be *essentia*, as He is conceived to
be the essence of all that is, yet strictly He is not *essentia*
(of which the contrary is *nihil*) but *super-essentia*[1]. Similarly
He is more-than-good, and more-than-goodness (ὑπεράγαθος,
ὑπεραγαθότης), more-than-eternal, and more-than-eternity
(ὑπεραιώνιος, ὑπεραιωνία). The use of phrases like these is
the attempt to unite the affirmation and the negation in
one statement, since the Absolute involves both the positive
and the negative. *Essentia est, affirmatio; essentia non est,*

[1] καὶ ὑπὲρ τὰ πάντα ἐστίν, ὡς πρὸ πάντων ὑπερουσίως ὑπερών. *De Div. Nom.*
v. 8 (824 B, Vol. 3, ed. Migne).

abdicatio; superessentialis est, affirmatio simul et abdicatio (462 C). But, as Erigena sees, every one of these attempts to express the nature of God by *super-* and ὑπερ- is really a negation. To say that God is superessential is not to say what He is, but what He is not[1]. *Nam qui dicit super-essentialis est, non, quid est, dicit, sed, quid non est; dicit enim essentiam non esse, sed plusquam essentiam* (462 D). God is indeed beyond all words, and all thought, for He surpasses all intellect, and is better known by not knowing, and is more truly denied in all things than affirmed (508) (684 D)[2].

Theophany. It is therefore one of Erigena's fundamental tenets that it is impossible to know God as He is. We know *that* He is, but not *what* He is. He is known to be only through the things He has created. That is, He is known only by Theophany (487 A). The sense which Erigena attaches to this phrase is not particularly clear or consistent. It seems generally to mean every manifestation of God through the medium of the creation. But it is only the devout soul that is prepared to receive the higher manifestations, and it is only to such souls that these are given. The words of Maximus are quoted as a definition of Theophany in the narrower sense. "As far as the human mind ascends in love, so far the divine wisdom descends in mercy (449 C)[3]." Theophany, therefore, in this more

---

[1] Wenn daher auch dem unmittelbaren Ausdruck nach keine Negation ist, so liegt die Negation doch dem Begriffe nach zu Grunde, nur die Form ist affirmativ, der Inhalt selbst aber negativ, und die negative Theologie erhält daher immer wieder das Uebergewicht über die affirmative. Wer von Gott sagt, dass er überwesentlich ist, sagt nicht, was er ist, sondern nur, was er nicht ist. Baur, *Lehre v. d. Dreieinigkeit*, XI. p. 276.

[2] Cf. Augustine, *De Ord.* II. 16. 44. *Enarr. in Ps. lxxxv.* 12.

[3] φασὶ γὰρ ἀλλήλων εἶναι παραδείγματα τὸν Θεὸν καὶ τὸν ἄνθρωπον, καὶ τοσοῦτον τῷ ἀνθρώπῳ τὸν Θεὸν διὰ φιλανθρωπίαν ἀνθρωπίζεσθαι, ὅσον ὁ ἄνθρωπος ἑαυτὸν τῷ Θεῷ δι' ἀγάπης δυνηθεὶς ἀπεθέωσε. *Ambigua* (1113 B, Vol. 91, ed. Migne).

restricted sense, is, on the part of man, an ascent to God in which every good desire and deed is a step, and on the part of God, a revelation of Himself to the human spirit in such fashion as our intelligence can understand.

The Nature of God. God is ἄναρχος, without beginning, without cause (516). Strictly, only the Father is ἄναρχος, since the Son and the Spirit have a *principium* in the Father (909 B)[1]. The essence of God is incomprehensible, as is the essence (οὐσία) of all that exists (451). But as our human intellect, which is one and invisible in itself, yet manifests itself in words and deeds, and expresses its thought in letters and figures[2], so the Divine Essence, which is far above the reach of our intellect, manifests itself in the created universe[3]. In this sense it may even be said to be created, in those things which are made by it and through it and in it (454 A), as the Apostle says that the Divine Nature is *made*, where the Word of God is born in the heart: *Who is made unto us wisdom from God and righteousness and sanctification and redemption* (1 Cor. i. 30). So the Divine Nature may be

[1] ὁ δὲ Υἱός, ἐὰν μὲν ὡς αἴτιον τὸν Πατέρα λαμβάνῃς, οὐκ ἄναρχος, ἀρχὴ γὰρ Υἱοῦ Πατὴρ ὡς αἴτιος· ἐὰν δὲ τὴν ἀπὸ χρόνου νοῇς ἀρχήν, καὶ ἄναρχος. Gregory Naz. *Orat.* 29.

[2] The metaphor is from Maximus: ἢ ὅτι δι' ἡμᾶς, τοὺς παχεῖς τὴν διάνοιαν, σωματωθῆναί τε δι' ἡμᾶς καὶ γράμμασι καὶ συλλαβαῖς καὶ φωναῖς τυπωθῆναι κατεδέξατο, ἵνα ἐκ πάντων τούτων ἡμᾶς ἑπομένους αὐτῷ κατὰ βραχὺ πρὸς ἑαυτὸν συναγάγῃ, ἑνοποιηθέντας τῷ πνεύματι.... *Ambigua* (1285–1288 A, Vol. 91, ed. Migne).

[3] Erigena derives Θεός from θεωρῶ, *video*, or from θέω, *curro*, since God sees all and runs through all. The second of these etymologies is ultimately from Plato, who represents Socrates (in the *Cratylus*, XVI. 397) as saying that the early Greeks "considered those only as gods, whom many of the barbarians at present regard as such—the sun, the moon, the earth, the stars, and the heavens. Now as they perceived all these moving and running round in a perpetual course, from this nature of running they called them gods" (ἀπὸ ταύτης τῆς φύσεως τῆς τοῦ θεῖν θεοὺς αὐτοὺς ἐπονομάσαι). Erigena, however, certainly got it from Gregory Nazianzen (*Orat.* XXX. 18) or some other of the Fathers.

said to create itself inasmuch as it creates from itself the nature of things.

God is infinite, and more than infinite : the infinitude of infinitudes (517 B). He is the similitude of the similar and the dissimilitude of the dissimilar: the opposite of opposites, and the contrary of contraries.

The Divine Nature is simplex, and more than simplex. We are not to think of the act of God as other than God Himself (518 A). There is no number in God[1], for He alone is *innumerabilis*; He is number without number, and as being beyond all number is the source of all number. It is not therefore one thing for God to be, and another for Him to will, and another for Him to create, but one and the same thing. These distinctions are not in God, but in our thought of God.

The Divine Nature and the Categories. A considerable part of the first book of Erigena's great work is taken up by the attempt to show in detail that the Aristotelian Categories are inapplicable to the nature of God. Erigena points out that four of the Ten Categories may be classed under Rest (*essentia, quantitas, situs, locus*), and six under Motion (*qualitas, relatio, habitus, tempus, agere, pati*) (469 A). He is aware that the categories are not beyond criticism, and he suggests the addition of possibility and impossibility (597 C)—an interesting anticipation of the categories of Kant. Erigena has little difficulty in showing that most of the categories can only apply to finite things. It is obvious that the nature of the Divinity must be beyond the limits of time and space, and the definition of quantity and quality. Erigena's real diffi-

---

[1] The thought is borrowed from Maximus: μονὰς δὲ μόνη κυρίως ἀκίνητος, ὅτι μήτε ἀριθμός ἐστι, μήτε ἀριθμητὸν ἢ ἀριθμούμενον (οὔτε γὰρ μέρος ἢ ὅλον ἢ σχέσις ἐστὶν ἡ μονὰς) καὶ κυρίως ἄναρχος....καὶ ἀρχὴ κυρίως, ὅτι παντὸς καὶ ἀριθμοῦ καὶ ἀριθμουμένου καὶ ἀριθμητοῦ αἰτία τυγχάνει. *Ambigua* (1185 B, Vol. 91, ed. Migne).

culty comes with the last categories, *agere* and *pati*. The Master says outright that God neither acts nor suffers, neither moves nor is moved, neither loves nor is loved. The Disciple naturally objects that the Scriptures plainly and frequently use such language of God (504 C). The Master replies that this is a condescension to the infirmity of our understanding, as the Apostle says: *I fed you with milk, not with meat* (1 Cor. iii. 2). That is alone properly called substance which is always the same: whatever varies proceeds from accidents (507 A). But God, as the ultimate substance, is immutable, and His nature has no accidents. As the supreme cause and the supreme principle of all, it is impossible that God should really act, or really suffer (508 C). The language of Scripture is intended for the instruction of simple souls, and, as a metaphorical use, is entirely justified. In so far as the categories of *agere* and *pati* may be used of God metaphorically *action* means that God wills all things to be, and *passion* that He loves all and would be loved by all (593 A). Love is the bond which binds all things together in an ineffable and indissoluble amity (519). It is the motion of things toward their final rest, which is also their first source. So God is rightly said to love, because He is the cause of love, and is diffused through all, and unites all, and the motion of love in all things ends in Him. The magnet, without moving, moves the iron to itself (520 B), and God, though He cannot strictly be said to love, is the source of the universal attraction and affinity that we call love.

The Divine Ignorance. The Divine Nature is the infinitude of infinities. God does not know, therefore, what He is. If He did know what He is, He would have defined Himself, and how is it possible to limit the infinite by definition? (586 C, D). The Disciple objects that if God does not, or cannot, define Himself, it would seem impossible to deny either ignorance or impotence of Him (587 B, C). The Master reminds the Disciple of the discussion of the categories, and of their inapplicability to God. God does not know *what* He is, because He is not a *what*. *Deus itaque nescit se, quid est, quia non est quid* (589 B). This ignorance surpasses all knowledge (590 D). It is not to be understood otherwise than as an infinite and incomprehensible knowledge. For in so far as God does not know Himself, as comprehended among things that are, He knows Himself as exalted beyond them (597 D).

There are three other species of the Divine ignorance. First, God does not know evil. The Divine knowledge of things is their cause. God does not know them because they are, but they are because God knows them. *Divina siquidem scientia omnium, quae sunt causa est. Non enim ideo Deus scit ea, quae sunt, quia subsistunt, sed ideo subsistunt, quia Deus ea scit*[1]. Hence, evil would really exist if God knew it. Second, God does not know anything of which the grounds (*rationes*) are not eternally created and known in Himself. Third, God does not know anything which has not yet appeared in action and effect (596 B, C).

The Trinity. The doctrine of the Trinity is not to Erigena merely a mysterious truth of revelation relating to the nature of the Deity, but a fundamental fact in the organisation of the universe. The Unity and the Trinity of God are not such a unity or such a trinity as can be understood

---

[1] This is directly from Augustine. "And with respect to all His creatures, both spiritual and corporeal, He does not know them because they are, but they are because He knows them (*non quia sunt, ideo novit, sed ideo sunt, quia novit*). For He was not ignorant what He was about to create, therefore He created because He knew; He did not know because He created" (*De Trin.* XV. 22). Compare Thomas Aquinas, *Summ. Theol.* I. qu. 14, art. 10.

by any created intelligence, whether human or angelic (456). The Unity is not to be conceived as singularity and sterility, rather it is the unity of a fertile multiplicity. The Trinity is the reciprocal relation within the Godhead. As Gregory Nazianzen said, answering the Eunomians, the name Father does not refer either to nature or to operation, *sed solius ad Filium habitudinis* (457 A)[1]. If it referred to nature, it would follow that the Father and the Son are of different natures; if it referred to operation, it would follow that the Son is a creature. But it connotes relation merely: the First Person of the Trinity is, in relation to the Second, the Father, and the Second Person is, in relation to the First, the Son[2]. The Spirit ineffably proceeds from (*ex*) the Father through (*per*) the Son (565 A). The Disciple asks expressly: Is the Father alone, or are the Father and the Son together the source (*causa*) of the Spirit[3]? The Master admits that there is densest darkness here, but proceeds to discuss the addition to the Nicene symbol.

The Filioque Clause. Some Greek Fathers, he reminds

---

[1] οὔτε οὐσίας, οὔτε ἐνεργείας, ἀλλὰ σχέσεως. *Ambigua* (1265 D, Vol. 91, ed. Migne).   [2] Augustine, *De Trin.* v. 5.

[3] The Greek theologians say that God the Father is the *cause* (αἰτία) of the Son and the Spirit—"an expression which has always sounded wrong to Latin theologians," as Dr Adrian Fortescue says (*The Orthodox Eastern Church*, p. 378). This is no doubt generally true. Thomas Aquinas, in discussing the Council of Florence, maintains that the Greeks use the term *causa* and the Latins only *principium*. *Apud Latinos non est consuetum, quod Pater dicatur causa Filii, vel Spiritus sancti, sed solum principium, vel auctor....Graeci, qui causae et causati nomine utuntur in divinis personis, non intendunt diversitatem naturae inducere, aut Filium esse creaturam; sed per hoc volunt ostendere solam originem personarum, sicut nos nomine principii* (*Contra errores Graecorum*, I.). But, as Bishop Pearson points out (*An Exposition of the Creed*, p. 59), there are many exceptions, as, for example, Augustine (*Lib. de Divers. Quaest.* LXXXIII. 16). *Deus omnium quae sunt causa est. Quod autem rerum omnium causa est, etiam sapientiae suae causa est, nec unquam Deus sine sapientia sua. Igitur sempiternae sapientiae suae causa est sempiterna.*

the Disciple, expound *et Filio* as *from* the Father *through* the Son (*a Patre per Filium*), and this is the form of doctrine which our philosopher favours. The Disciple enquires again whether the Son is begotten and the Spirit proceeds from the essence or from the substance of the Father? (613 A). The Master replies that this is easily resolved if you recall the difference, as expounded by Dionysius, Gregory Nazianzen, and Maximus, between the essence and the substance of God. Οὐσία, *essentia*, is the one, simplex nature of the Deity. Ὑπόστασις, *substantia*, is the individual substance and proper character (*proprium*) of the Persons (613 A, B). (Erigena breaks off here to explain that while the Greek Fathers used to say, μίαν οὐσίαν ἐν τρίσιν ὑποστάσεσιν, One Essence in Three Substances, Augustine and other Latin Fathers say One Substance in Three Persons[1]. The difference, he remarks, is merely verbal: the faith is the same though the words vary.) Now the essence of God is the one common nature of the Three Persons, and if the Son is begotten of this nature and the Father is not begotten of it, that is the same as to say that the Father is not (614 A)—that He does not subsist at all, if He does not subsist in the same way as the Son, for the Three Persons must obviously stand in the same relation to the nature which is common to the Three. It is therefore not of the essence, but of the substance of the Father that the Son is begotten and the Spirit proceeds. So among men sons are not begotten of the common nature of humanity, but of the proper nature of the father. But in all our thoughts of the Trinity, we are reminded, we deal with mere traces of the truth, and not with the truth itself, which surpasses the understanding of every creature.

[1] Cf. Augustine, *De Trin.* v. 10, and VII. 7.

Christology. Apart from what is involved in his treatment of the Trinity, and later of the Resurrection, there is not much specially Christological doctrine in Erigena's work. Perhaps the only other points are two, concerned with the relation of the two natures in Christ, and with the relation of the Holy Spirit to Christ's earthly manifestation. Erigena teaches that Christ is impassible in His Divinity: it is only in His humanity that He can suffer. Yet the one substance of the Word and of His humanity is not separated in His Passion, for the humanity of Christ suffers (*passus*) and His Divinity sympathises with it (*compassus*) (745 A)[1]—a paradoxical expression which recalls Tennyson's lines: "How is it? Canst thou feel for me Some painless sympathy with pain?"

Elsewhere there is a passage which sets forth a doctrine beloved by the mystics, that as in the fecundity of the Divine Nature (*fecunditatem divinam*) the Spirit proceeds from the Father through the Son, and as in the assumption of flesh the Son is conceived and born of the Spirit, so also, through the Spirit, Christ is daily conceived and born and nourished in the womb of faith, as in the body of a most chaste mother (611 C, D). There is also the remark in another place that the Incarnation benefited man by way of redemption, and the angels by way of knowledge (912 C).

Creation. The act, or rather the process of creation, is consistently conceived as mediated through Christ, but this scarcely involves any doctrine that deserves to be called Christological. There is no personal or historical conception involved: the Logos is no more than a metaphysical formula

---

[1] The thought is borrowed from Epiphanius: ὁ Λόγος σὰρξ γενόμενος, οὐ πάσχων ἐν τῇ θεότητι, συμπάσχων δὲ μετὰ τῆς ἀνθρωπότητος. *De Fide* (ἀγκυρωτός), XCII. (185 C, Vol. 43, ed. Migne).

used to express the unity of the primordial causes[1]. The process of creation must be conceived in the light of the truth that with God to be and to will and to act are one and the same thing. We distinguish His existence from His will and His will from His action, but the distinction is in our own minds, and not in the nature of God, which is one and simplex. It is not therefore one thing for God to be and another thing for Him to create. Nor is it one thing for Him to see, and another to will, and another to act (518 A). The whole act of creation is in the words: *And God saw that it was good* (Gen. i. 25). When God sees the creation, it exists, and it exists in Him, for nothing exists that does not exist in Him and He sees nothing but Himself. *Visio Dei totius universitatis est conditio. Non enim aliud est ei videre, et aliud facere, sed visio illius voluntas ejus est, et voluntas operatio...Non enim Deus vidit nisi seipsum, quia extra ipsum nihil est, et omne, quod in ipso est, ipse est, simplexque visio ipsius est, et a nullo alio formatur ipsa nisi a seipso* (704 B, C).

That God creates all, means that He is in all, that He is the essence of all. He alone really exists, *per se*, and all that really is, in the whole of existence, is God. Nothing of all that exists, in other words, exists of itself.

All things were created at once, though the act of creation is narrated in order of time (807 B). Nothing is before or after with God, for there is no past or future with Him, nor any medium between past and future, but all is at once to Him. *Animadverte quod Deo nihil est ante, nihil post, cui*

---

[1] This is a very ancient thought. "The Son is neither absolutely one, as one; nor yet many, as parts; but one, as all things; for from Him are all things; and He is the circle of all powers collected and united into one." Clement of Alexandria, *Stromata*, IV. 635. 9. Cf. Origen, *De Princ.* I. 2.

*nihil praeteritum, nihil futurum, nihil medium inter prae-
teritum et futurum, quoniam ipsi omnia simul sunt.* Why,
then, should not God make all things at once, which, in
order to make, He saw and willed at once? It is obvious
that the Scriptures must narrate the act of creation part
by part, though it happened altogether and at once, as
we are compelled to express a single instantaneous thought
in a series of temporally separated sounds and spatially
separated letters (708 C). The creation is coessential and
coeternal with God. For if God existed before the universe, then the creation is an "accident" (517 A), i.e. God
is then regarded as the primal "substance" and the creation
as an "accident" of that "substance." But God has no
"accidents"; His nature is simplex and immutable.

Elsewhere Erigena says that all is eternal in the Wisdom
of the Father, yet not strictly coeternal with the Father, for
the artist precedes his art, and the art precedes the things
that are made by it (635, 636). What Erigena is here concerned to posit, is the logical priority of God as the First
Cause. He would have said, in Augustine's manner, that
there is no question of temporal priority, since time only
begins with the world, and until the world exists there
is no before or after.

God precedes the world, not in time, but in reason, since
He is the cause of all, and is Himself uncaused (909 A);
and all exists, causatively, in Him from all eternity. Whatever is, is only in so far as the rational grounds of it eternally
subsist in God (640).

If the creative Wisdom were taken away from all that is,
all would revert to absolute nothingness; no existence, life,
sense, reason, intellect, or goodness would remain. All
things, therefore, considered absolutely in themselves, are

nothing, as Augustine has said: *Et inspexi cetera intra te, et vidi, nec omnino esse, nec omnino non esse. Nec omnino esse, quia non sunt quod tu es, nec omnino non esse, quia a te sunt*[1].

This world is therefore nothing: only the things that are before and after this world are eternal (561 A) (and only these really exist).

Why did God create anything? That the universe might exist to His praise, for there is no creature that does not, either in itself or through another, praise the Supreme Goodness. Moreover, since God is good, He could not refrain from the creation of what is good—good, that is, not in and through itself, but in and through Him. Again, God would not have been actually the Lord of all, the Creator of all, the Judge of all, if He had created nothing (952 B).

Creation Ex Nihilo. All was created out of nothing, but we are not to understand by nothing the absolute privation of essence, substance, and accidents, mere nothingness, *nihil de nihilo*, but the excellence of the Divine superessentiality (634 B). That is to say: God created all things out of nothing, is a precisely equivalent statement to: God created all things out of Himself.

The nothing of which the world is created, then, is not mere privation of being. How could privation of relation exist before any relation existed, or negation of existence before existence? But if *nihil* be taken to signify not merely the privation of habitude or the absence of existence, but the total negation of habitude, existence, substance, accidents, and of all that can be said or thought, then it necessarily means God, Who is the negation of all that is, as being utterly beyond all that is (686).

The Divine Goodness, as above all, is said not to be (*non*

[1] *Conf.* VII. 11.

esse); as in all, it is said to be, because it is the essence, substance, genus, species, quality, quantity, time, space, and so forth, of the whole universe. It is all that is in every creature (681 D).

So God makes all of nothing, that is, He produces of His super-existence, existence; of His super-life, life; of His super-intellect, intellect; and of the negation of all that is and is not, the affirmation of all that is and is not (683 B).

The nothing, then, of which all is made is the ineffable, incomprehensible, inaccessible brightness of the Divine Goodness, unknown to all human and all angelic intelligence, for it is supernatural and superessential, and, when thought of by itself, neither is, nor was, nor shall be (680 D), and by reason of its utter incomprehensibility is rightly called nothing. When it appears in theophanies it issues from nothing (*ex nihilo*) into something (*in aliquid*). What is beyond all existence appears in existence, and is a theophany, *divina apparitio*. It appears first of all by means of the primal causes, in which it is made a formless matter—matter, because it is the beginning of the existence of things; formless, because nearest to the formlessness of the Divine Wisdom. This is properly called formless, because it is superior to all forms, and yet it is the exemplar of all forms (681 A, C).

The corporeal is constituted by the incorporeal. Therefore the corporeal is not made of nothing, but of something. *Corpora ergo non de nihilo, sed de aliquo fiunt.* Corporeal things are constituted from quantity, quality, species, colours, length, breadth, height, space and time. When these are taken away bodies do not exist; when these are compounded, there are bodies, whether general elements, or the most specialised forms of corporeal things.

The Disciple suggests that at least the general elements are made of nothing? The Master replies: Then what of the primordial causes? If bodies are made of elements, and elements of nothing, then nothing is not nothing, but a cause. And it follows either that the Word of God (in Whom all causes exist) is nothing (which in that sense is impious, for the sense in which the Word of God is called *nihil* is not *per privationem substantiae* but *per excellentiam naturae*), or that there is another cause, beside the Word of God, called nothing, of which God made all things (663). All things corporeal are therefore made of something (*de aliquo*) and not of nothing (*de nihilo*). Are the primal causes, then, made of nothing in the Word of God, or were they always in Him? They were always in Him; there never was a time when they were not. How then could they be made of nothing? If it is said, the nothing of which they were made always was, and they were always made of it, then where was that nothing always? If in the Word of God, then it was not nothing, but a great something (*magnum aliquid*), for all that is in the Word really and naturally subsists, and is numbered among the primal causes. If beyond the Word of God, then you postulate two opposed sources (*principia*) and are become a Manichaean (464).

What is Created is Eternal. We may say that all things always were, and always were not. For they always were, *causaliter*, in the Word of God, beyond space and time, beyond quantity and quality, beyond all forms and species known either to intellect or to sense. And they always were not, before they issued forth in space and time, and the other forms of conditioned existence. They were not locally or temporally, or in generation. So there is no created thing of which it may not be said that it always was, always is, and always shall be, and, equally, that it always was not, always is not, and always shall not be. It is always known to God, and always beyond the knowledge of the creature, and therefore is to God and is not to us. Then it appears in space and time, in quantity and quality, and therefore is to us, and is not to God (665). For in so far as things exist in these accidents, they do not really exist, and do not always exist (*nec tamen vere, nec semper sunt*) (666 A, B). All, therefore, that is of God, is both eternal in the Word of God, and made in the Word of God: the making does not precede the eternity, nor the eternity the making (669 A).

The Disciple cannot understand how all things can be both eternal and made (638 C). Is not *made* the contradiction of *eternal*? How can anything be eternal, which is not, before it is made? What begins to be in time, how can it be in eternity? For what is eternal neither begins to be nor ceases to be (636 A).

The Master asks whether God is capable of accidents[1]? No. Then the creation of the world is not an accident. Therefore God was not before the creation of the world. Otherwise the creation of the world is an accident (639 A, B) (that is, God is conceived as a primal "substance," existing prior to that "accident"—that attribute or modification or consequence of the primal substance—which we call the creation).

The Disciple still cannot understand how all things can be both eternal and created, unless, according to the teaching of Dionysius, in the sense that God is both the maker of all, and is made in all, and this seems to lead to the monstrous conclusion: *Deus itaque omnia est, et omnia Deus!* (650 D).

[1] Augustine, *De Trin.* v. 6.

The Master in reply enquires if the Disciple is acquainted with the science of arithmetic, and asks if all numbers are not *causaliter* and *aeternaliter* in the monad? (651 A). Thence they extend by multiplication into infinity. All equalities have their source in the number two; all inequalities in the number three; and all species originate from equality and inequality (654 B). Six is the number of the days of creation because six is the multiple of the first equal number and the first unequal number; and it is the first number that is made up of its own parts, for it is the sum of one, two, and three, which are the sixth, the third, and the half of itself (656 B)[1].

Now what always remains is eternal, and the grounds (*rationes*) of numbers are eternal, for they always remain in the monad (655 A). Numbers, therefore, are both eternal and made—eternal in the monad, made in their multiplication from the monad. Similarly, all things are both eternal and made—eternal in God and made in the creation.

The acts of the Divine Will and what God makes are one and the same (673 D). If not, the will of God is separated

---

[1] Erigena borrowed this from Augustine: "And this number is on this account called perfect, because it is completed in its own parts: for it has these three, sixth, third, and half; nor is there any other part found in it, which we can call an aliquot part. The sixth part of it, then, is one; the third part, two; the half, three. But one and two and three complete the same six. And Holy Scripture commends to us the perfection of this number, especially in this, that God finished His works in six days, and on the sixth day man was made in the image of God" (*De Trin.* IV. 7). There is a similar passage in *De Civ. Dei*, XI. 30. Augustine probably has got the thought from Philo, who says (*De Mundi Opificio*, 2. 1. 2 : 3. 1. 3) that the six days of creation refer not to time, but to order, and that six is the most productive of numbers and the most perfect. For it is the product of the first odd (or male) number, three, and the first even (or female) number, two. And it is the first number that is equal in its parts, and completed from them, for it is the sum of one-half (three), one-third (two), and one-sixth (one), of itself.

from God and annexed to created things, so that God is one,
and the will of God is another—that is, God is then the
maker of His will and His will is the thing made. If the
will of God is not beyond (*extra*) His nature, and if with
Him to will and to do are the same (674 A), then God, when
He creates, creates Himself. All therefore that God wills
and sees and makes is coeternal with Himself, yet so that
He, since He is superessential, is one, and what He creates
in Himself is another. God alone really and properly is in
all things, and nothing really and properly is, which is not
God (675 B, C). The world is therefore a theophany, an
appearance of Him of Whom and through Whom and unto
Whom are all things.

Nothing really exists, therefore, in the whole creation but
God. He alone really is, and all else is, in the degree in
which it participates in Him. Do you deny, asks the Master,
that the Creator and the creation are one? It is not easy to
deny it, the Disciple answers, indeed, to resist this conclusion
seems to me absurd (528 B).

But this essential unity of the Creator and the creation
does not deny the distinction between the superexistence of
God, which surpasses all thought, and the existence of the
world of appearance. How does this last come to be at all?
How does the One manifest itself as the Many? and the
spiritual reveal itself in the material?

The Primal Causes. The answer of Erigena is given
largely by his doctrine of the *causae primordiales*. These
primal causes, of which the Logos is the unity and the
aggregate, are a kind of medium between God and the
creature (*quae medietatem quandam inter Deum et creaturam
obtinent*) (683 A). They are called πρωτότυπα, *primordialia
exempla*, προορίσματα, *predestinationes vel definitiones*, θεῖα

θελήματα, *divinae voluntates*, ἰδέαι, *species vel formae*[1] (529). The first words of Scripture: *In the beginning (in principio) God made the heaven and the earth* (Gen. i. 1) mean that God created (*creavit*) the primordial causes in the Son before the world was made (*ante omnia, quae condita sunt*). By *heaven* the intelligible world is meant; by *earth* the sensible world (545, 546).

What difference is there, asks the Disciple, between these primordial causes and formless matter? The Master answers: To be, and not to be, are absolute contraries. Now nothing is nearer proper being (*vere esse*) than the created causes of created things, but nothing is nearer proper non-being (*non vere esse*) than formless matter, for, as Augustine says, *informe prope nihil*. There is therefore the greatest difference between what is near to real being (*vera essentia*) and what is next to the privation of real being, that is, next to nothing (546).

But the earth was *without form and void* (Gen. i. 2). How can the exemplars of corporeal nature, which were perfect in God, as created (*condidit*) by the Father in the Son before the sensible world existed, be called *vacuum et inane*? Because sensible things in their effects were wanting (*vacabat*), and because there was no quantity, nor corporeal mass, nor dispersed space (549). *Darkness was upon the face of the deep* (Gen. i. 2)—upon the abyss of the primordial causes, for

---

[1] πολλῷ γε μᾶλλον ἐπὶ τῆς καὶ αὐτοῦ καὶ πάντων αἰτίας, προϋφεστάναι τὰ πάντα τῶν ὄντων παραδείγματα, κατὰ μίαν ὑπερούσιον ἔνωσιν συγχωρητέον· ἐπεὶ καὶ οὐσίας παράγει κατὰ τὴν ἀπὸ οὐσίας ἔκβασιν. παραδείγματα δέ φαμεν εἶναι τοὺς ἐν Θεῷ τῶν ὄντων οὐσιοποιοὺς καὶ ἑνιαίως προϋφεστῶτας λόγους, οὓς ἡ θεολογία προόρισμοὺς καλεῖ, καὶ θεῖα καὶ ἀγαθὰ θελήματα, τῶν ὄντων ἀφοριστικὰ καὶ ποιητικά, καθ' οὓς ὁ ὑπερούσιος τὰ ὄντα πάντα καὶ προώρισε καὶ παρήγαγεν. *De Div. Nom.* v. 8 (*ad fin.*) (824 C, Vol. 3, ed. Migne).

This passage in Dionysius is undoubtedly the source of Erigena's doctrine of the *causae primordiales*, and that doctrine is by far the most important of our philosopher's debts to the Areopagite.

before numbers of spiritual essences proceeded from it, no created intellect could know that they were (550). The wisdom of God, in which all things are created, and really subsist, and beyond which nothing can be known to be, remains in Him invisible and incomprehensible, *lux inaccessibilis* (551), light that is darkness to every created mind[1]. The primal causes remain in the wisdom of God, and are invisible in themselves, and so are *darkness*, but appear in their effects in the sensible world, and so are *light* (552 A).

The primal causes are in a sense coeternal with the Word, in Whom they are eternally created by the Father, and with the Father, Who is coeternal with the Word (561 B). But only in a sense. For Erigena maintains a difference between the Logos and all that exists in Him. He says expressly elsewhere that nothing is coeternal or coessential with the Son except the Father and the Spirit: *et nihil ei coaeternum vel consubstantiale intelligitur vel coessentiale praeter suum Patrem et suum Spiritum a Patre per ipsum procedentem*[2]. The primal causes are eternally created in the Logos, and in that sense they are coeternal with the Logos, since they always exist in God without temporal beginning. But they are not, in the full sense, coeternal with God (*non omnino tamen Deo esse coaeternas*), because they have their source in the Creator and not in themselves. He is the Creator and they are the created, and the dependent relation has always existed. True eternity belongs to God alone, since He, without beginning or end, Himself is the beginning and end of all (562 A). The Father creates all things in the Son, and perfects all things by the Spirit. The Father is the source (*causa*) of the Son and of the Spirit; the Son is the cause

---

[1] Dionysius, *Epist. ad Dorotheam* (1073 A, Vol. 3, ed. Migne), and *De Mystica Theologia*, II. 1 (1025 A, Vol. 3, ed. Migne).   [2] *Homil.* 287 D.

of the archetypal causes which were created in Him by the Father (*causa est conditionis principaliter causarum*); the Spirit is the cause of the distribution of the causes created by the Father in the Son (*causarum distributionis Spiritus sanctus causa est*) in their general and special effects (601 B).

The special work (*proprium*) of the Spirit is thus, speaking theologically, the administration of the Gospel of the Incarnation (562 D); speaking more generally, the distribution and division of all that the Father creates in the Son into fruitful multiplicity—the distribution of causes in their effects, and the division of these in genera, species and number (566 A, B). What the Father wills (*vult*), He creates (*condit*) in the Son, and distributes (*distribuit*) in the Spirit (579 D). Yet the inseparable operation of the Divine Unity is not segregated: what the Father does, that the Son does and that the Spirit does (566 C).

A real cause contains within itself the most perfect reality of that of which it is the cause (571 A). The primordial causes are what the Greeks call ideas, that is, *species vel formae aeternae et incommutabiles rationes*: according to which and in which all the universe, visible and invisible, is formed and ruled (615). As Dionysius teaches, they are providential powers, issuing from God, by participation in which all existing things exist[1]. These powers participate in Being, and so first are, and then are sources of further existences. The self-existent Life is the source of all that lives, as living; the self-existent Unity is the source of all that is united, as united; and so forth. These primal causes are goodness, existence (*essentia*), life, wisdom, truth, intelligence (*intellectus*), reason, virtue, justice, health (*salus*),

[1] *De Div. Nom.* v. 11.

greatness (*magnitudo*), omnipotence, eternity, peace,—each conceived *per seipsam*,—and all the primal powers (*virtutes*) and rational grounds (*rationes*) which the Father created, all together and at once, in the Son, and which reach throughout the whole creation. Whatever is good is good by participation in the self-existent Good ; whatever subsists essentially and substantially, subsists by participation in the self-existent Existence (616), and so with the rest.

Later on in his work Erigena gives another list of primal causes that does not exactly correspond with this list— Goodness, Existence, Life, Reason, Intelligence, Wisdom, Virtue, Happiness, Truth, Eternity, with the addition of Greatness, Love, Peace, Unity, and Perfection (622–3). The primal causes are intended to derive from one another. Goodness is more universal than Being, since both Being and non-Being (in Erigena's familiar sense) participate in Goodness. So Being is a wider conception than Life, for both living and non-living things participate in Being. So Reason is dependent upon Life, and Happiness upon Virtue, though it is difficult to see how the gradation and the dependence can be extended to Truth and Eternity.

The primal causes extend to infinity (*in infinitum protendantur*), since the Creator is infinite, from Whom and through Whom and in Whom they exist (623 D). In themselves the primal causes are one, simplex, and not known in a defined order, or separated into a series. We know them as multiple and serial only as we know them in their effects. The monad is one, and only one, and it is not one as compounded from a multitude, but one in itself, and yet numbers to infinity proceed from it (624). All lines unite in a point, and are indistinguishable in it, and yet all proceed from it (625). So the primal causes subsist uniformly and unalterably in the Word, in Whom they are created, eternally one and the same, beyond all order and all number. They remain unknown until they manifest themselves in theophanies, and in these they are divided and multiplied, and an infinity of effects proceeds from them. But the order and the number are not in the primal causes themselves but in our minds (626).

Erigena has a special reason, and a thoroughly Platonic one, for placing Goodness first among the primal causes— that Goodness is the highest possible idea. God, Who is creative goodness, first of all creates goodness in Himself, and then through it, creates all that is[1]. Hence all that is, is in so far as it is good; in so far as it is not good, or less good, it is not. If the good were wholly abstracted from existence, this would cease to be: nothing would remain.

Creative Goodness. Goodness is essentially creative: evil is essentially destructive. Evil corrupts the things that exist and seeks to destroy them. If it were possible for evil to succeed absolutely, it would mean that all would perish, and evil would perish along with all else (511). But it is the property of the Divine Goodness to call the non-existent into existence. *Divinae siquidem bonitatis proprium est, quae non erant, in essentiam vocare.* Goodness is not in point of origin an attribute of Being, but Being of Goodness (627). *Non enim per essentiam introducta est bonitas, sed per boni-tatem introducta est essentia.* To speak of being, unless it means the being of good, is an abuse of language. We cannot reverse the argument and say that if existence were taken away, goodness would not remain, for it is not only things that are, that are good, but things that are not (*quae non sunt*) are also called good. So that Goodness is a much

---

[1] Cf. Augustine, *De Civ. Dei*, XI. 21.

more general term than Being, for one species of goodness
is in the things that are, and another in the things that are
not. Goodness, therefore, is a kind of genus of Existence,
and Existence a kind of species of Goodness. So Goodness
is the genus of Life (628), and Life the genus of Reason.
Reason divides into two species—Wisdom (*sapientia*) and
Knowledge (*scientia*)[1]. Wisdom, whether in angels or in men,
contemplates divine, eternal and unchangeable things. Knowledge contemplates the things of Nature which proceed from
the primal causes by generation, and are divided into genera
and species, and characterised by differences and properties,
and subject to space and time.

Wisdom and Knowledge participate in Reason. Both
rational and irrational things participate in Life. Both
things that live and things that do not live participate
in Existence. Both things that are and things that are not
participate in Goodness (629)[2].

The Disciple asks: What is the difference between the
primal causes and substances? The Master answers: The
primal causes are the most general grounds (*rationes*) of
being constituted in the Word of God. The substances
are the separate and special properties and grounds (*rationes*)
of being of separate and special things as distributed and
constituted in their causes.

The world proceeds from these causes and substances,
being compounded of the qualities of substances, into which
it will finally be resolved again (887 A, B). Yet the qualities
do not leave the substances, but inseparably adhere to them

---

[1] Cf. Augustine, *De Trin.* XII. 25.

[2] καὶ γὰρ ἡ τἀγαθοῦ θεωνυμία τὰς ὅλας τοῦ πάντων αἰτίου προόδους ἐκφαίνουσα,
καὶ εἰς τὰ ὄντα, καὶ εἰς τὰ οὐκ ὄντα ἐκτείνεται, καὶ ὑπὲρ τὰ ὄντα καὶ ὑπὲρ τὰ οὐκ
ὄντα ἐστίν. *De Div. Nom.* V. 1 (816 B, Vol. 3, ed. Migne).

(886 D), and the substances do not leave the primal causes, and the primal causes do not leave the Word of God (886 C).

Are the primal causes and the substances creatures? Not properly; we mean by creatures, generally, what exists by generation, in species, and in time. What was before time and is beyond space is not properly called a creature, though such things may be called creatures when we regard their existence as *post Deum* (888 A).

Matter. Material things have therefore an immaterial origin in the primal causes. Further, material things are immaterial in their constitution, when once they are defined and analysed. A point, in which lines begin and end, is neither a line nor a part of a line, but the end of lines. The space (*locus*) of a point is not a space perceived by the senses, but a space understood by the intellect. So a point is incorporeal, and the beginning of lines; a line is incorporeal and the beginning of surfaces; a surface is incorporeal and the beginning of solidity, and solidity is the perfection of matter. Matter, therefore, is really a combination of incorporeal qualities. It is form which con tutes and contains all material bodies, and form is incorporeal (484). Matter, apart from form, could not be known by the senses (499 B). As Gregory of Nyssa says, matter consists of qualities, and if these are taken away, it cannot be known. That is not body (*corpus*) which lacks existence, and shape (*figura*), and solidity, and difference, and weight, and so forth. None of these qualities is body; each is something beyond and apart from body, but when they are found together (*concurrent*) there is constituted corporeal substance (502). If they are taken away, there is left only formless matter, which, as Augustine says, is merely the mutability

of mutable things, which is capable of receiving all forms[1].
So Plato teaches in the *Timaeus* that formless matter is
merely the capacity of form. So also Dionysius says that
matter participates in ornament and beauty and form, and
that without these, matter is formless, and cannot be known
(500). Matter, therefore, is formed out of a concourse of
immaterial qualities, as shadows are formed out of light
and bodies; yet neither light nor body is changed into
shadow, and when the shadow disappears, it returns into
its causes, that is, into light and body (501).

Forms and colours are incorporeal. Nothing that the eye
can see can be known to sense except in form and colour.
Yet form and colour cannot appear of themselves, but only
as attached to matter, and matter, without form and colour,
is invisible and incorporeal (662 C, D). Therefore the corporeal is constituted by the concourse of the incorporeal
(663 A).

Formlessness precedes form, not in time, but in natural
order, as the cause precedes the effect. So the voice and
the word issue from the mouth at once, yet the voice
precedes the word, not in time, but as the cause of the
word. And so formlessness in all things preceded form,
causally, not temporally, for both together and at once
(*simul et semel*) were brought out of nothing into existence
by the will of the Creator (647 A) (599 B).

All corporeal and sensible things are constituted of matter
and form. Matter without form, formless matter, is *invisibilis et incomposita, seu inanis et vacua* (Gen. i. 2, *LXX* and
Vulgate) (548 B).

Body is not a quantity of οὐσία but a *quantum*, and colour
is not a quality of οὐσία but a *quale* in a *quantum*. In Nature,

[1] *Conf.* XII. 5.

quantity and quality and οὐσία are always associated; these three are found in all natural bodies, but it is only in our intellect that they are separated (483 A, C). Οὐσία is discerned only by the intellect; it is never visible. Quantity and quality are also invisible in οὐσία but they break forth into visibility in *quantum* and *quale*, when, conjoining themselves, they compose the sensible body (495 C).

Form. Form in οὐσία and form in quality are to be distinguished. Forms in οὐσία (which Erigena elsewhere calls forms of substance) (502 B) are substantial species. Substantial form is not more in the many or less in the few, but it is all in one and one in all. The substantial form of man was in the first man, and in all men. It is human nature, which is found in all men, and is alike in all men. The differences between men are not due to nature, in this sense, but to generation, quantity, quality, time and space (703 A, C).

But forms in quality are what we usually call forms in natural bodies or figures in geometry. The form of man, in this sense, is his erect posture, as distinguished from the bent posture of animals, which is their form (494 A, D).

The Elements. The four simple elements (named from the four greatest bodies composed of them) are Fire, Air, Water, Earth. They are invisible, incomprehensible, universally diffused (701 B). All sensible things are constituted by the proportionate union of these elements, not the direct union of the elements themselves, which are indissoluble and incorruptible, but the union of their qualities, in proportion and in opposition. These qualities are four; heat, humidity, cold, dryness (604 C). Heat and cold are active; humidity and dryness are passive (712). These four qualities and the four elements in which they inhere are a kind of intermediary between the primordial causes and composite bodies (713 B).

It may be remarked here that Erigena devotes two or three chapters to the natural science of his day, in which he is largely dependent on Pliny the Elder. He has some quaint remarks about the chastity of the gryphon and the filial piety of the stork, and he finds occasion to mention the recognition of Ulysses by his dog after twenty years of absence. The bulk of the section, however, is devoted to astronomy, and there is one point of special interest in this.

Astronomy. He believes the earth to be the centre of the universe, of course, but thinks that the four planets, Mercury, Venus, Mars and Jupiter, circle round the sun, which is midway between the earth and the sphere of the fixed stars. The distances between the heavenly bodies are all of a regular arithmetical proportion, and this fits in with the doctrine of the harmony of the spheres, which Erigena accepts. The unit of distance is the earth's diameter, and this space is the equivalent of one tone. There is a space equal to one terrestrial diameter between the surface of the earth and the centre of the moon; another from the centre of the moon to the orbit of the planets; another from the orbit of the planets to the centre of the sun; another from the centre of the sun to the further side of the planetary orbit; another from there to Saturn (which does not, like the rest of the planets, circle round the sun, but directly round the earth); another from Saturn to the sphere of the fixed stars. These six spaces, with the diameter of the earth itself for a seventh, give the tones of the octave. The radii of the lunar orbit, of the solar orbit, and of the orbit of the sphere of the fixed stars, are thus three times, seven times, and thirteen times the length of the radius of the circumference of the earth.

It has been pointed out that this is decidedly the most advanced astronomical scheme of the Middle Ages, and that, except for the exemption of Saturn, it is the system of Tycho Brahe[1].

Time and Space. The whole world, as it now exists, exists in space and time, and could not exist without them (468). All that is, except God, is known as in space and in time. It is the doctrine of Gregory Nazianzen that space and time always exist together, and could not be understood apart (481 C). Space and time are to be understood as before all things that exist, for that which contains is necessarily thought of before that which is contained. Space and time will cease, when all things are in God, and the blessed will be like Melchizedek, having neither beginning of days nor end of life (482). Space is natural definition, and mode and position (483 C). Time is the motion of things in generation which pass out of non-existence into existence (483 C). Nothing that is created is immobile. And all movement is a part of the universal movement from non-existence to existence,—the motion which seeks its end in God, and then rests in Him (514). Time and Nature were created together (513 B). But time is logically prior. There are two great errors that beset the mind of man, as Augustine has said, to think of space as *supra caelum* and of time as *ante mundum* (888 C). There can be no movement when no part of the world is moved, and no time when there is no movement to be measured (890 B).

Time and space are always conceived as conditions of

---

[1] Duhem, *Le Système du Monde*, III. p. 62; Dreyer, *Planetary Systems*, p. 363.

existence, rather than as categories of knowledge. Yet
Erigena's uncompromising idealism regards being as secondary to knowledge.

Knowledge. The knowledge (*intellectus*) of all is all, for
it alone knows all. The knowledge of all is logically prior
to the existence of all (632 D), and He who knows all, knows
nothing beyond Himself, for there is nothing beyond Himself. All that we know is theophany, and subsists in God.
All that is known and all that is felt is but an appearance
of what does not appear, a manifestation of what is hidden
an affirmation of the negation, a comprehension of the
incomprehensible, an utterance of the unutterable, an access
to the inaccessible, an understanding of the unintelligible,
an embodiment of the incorporeal, an essence of the superessential, a form of the formless, a measure of the measureless,
a number of the numberless, a definition of the infinite
(*infiniti definitio*).

Our own intellect is an example of this, for it is invisible
and incomprehensible, and yet it is manifested and comprehended by signs, such as letters and words. And, while it is
thus manifested, it remains in itself unseen, silent, incorporeal,
though it makes itself seen and heard, and incorporates itself,
in its words and deeds (633).

The essence of all things is nothing but the knowledge of
them in the mind of God. *Nihil enim est aliud omnium
essentia, nisi omnium in divina sapientia cognitio* (559 B).
Intellectus enim omnium in Deo essentia omnium est (559 B).
More generally, intellect is the essence of things. *Intellectus
enim rerum veraciter ipsae res sunt*, or, as Dionysius says,
Cognitio earum, quae sunt, ea quae sunt, est (535 B, D).

The act of knowledge is an act of creation; to understand
is to create (579 D). The Disciple asks what difference

there is, then, between the operation of the uncreated and creating Trinity, and that of the created and creating trinity? i.e. between the creative knowledge of God, and the creative knowledge of the human mind? (580 A). The Master answers that the difference is that God creates out of nothing (581 A). Elsewhere Erigena distinguishes the creative knowledge of God as *causaliter* and that of man as *effectualiter* (779 C).

What we know of things, whether by sense or by intellect, we may be said to create, for, when we know things, we draw them into ourselves, and compare and divide and unify them (765 C). In so far as the intellect really knows, it becomes what it knows. *Qui enim pure intelligit in eo, quod intelligit, fit* (780 B).

The Trinity in Creation. We have before remarked that the doctrine of the Trinity is to Erigena the leading principle of creation. It is the *essentia* of the Father, the *sapientia* of the Son and the *vita* of the Spirit, that are the source of the existence of all, of the wisdom which is manifest in the order of the universe, and of life in all its manifestations (455 C). The Father wills, the Son creates, the Spirit perfects (553 D).

In every rational and intellectual nature there are three inseparable and incorruptible *manentia*: οὐσία, δύναμις, ἐνέργεια, *essentia, virtus, operatio* (486 B). No man can say what οὐσία is. It is simplex, indivisible, incomprehensible either by sense or by intellect. It can only be known through space and time, which inseparably adhere to it in the creation, for all things created are local and temporal; local inasmuch as they are not limitless; and temporal inasmuch as they begin to be. We can therefore only know of anything *that* it is (*quia est*), but not *what* it is (*quid est*) (487 A). Hence, οὐσία is to be thought of as a sort of unknown centre of being, which is inferred from the existence of its periphery of things in space and time.

All things partake of οὐσία but all things do not partake of it equally. Some have more of it and some less, but nothing that exists is entirely deprived of participation in it (505 D). It is by this participation that everything exists. But within each class of existence, οὐσία is equally present in all, not more in the whole or less in the part; not more in all men or less in one man (492 A).

The trinity of *essentia, virtus, operatio*, is found in all substances, whether possessed of bodies or not. It is one thing to be, another to be able to act, and another to act. A tree exists, and can grow, and does grow. A man is, and has power to understand, and does understand. Every creature, visible and invisible, has within it this triad of existence, potentiality, and action. And these three are one, and not a composite one, but a most simplex and inseparable unity (881 A, B).

When I say *I know that I am*, three inseparable things are signified in the one statement—I prove that I am, that I can know that I am, and that I do know that I am. *Essentia, virtus, actio* are all involved in it (490 B).

The Trinity in Man. The soul of man has a triune character, distinguished as intellect (νοῦς), reason (λόγος) and sense (διάνοια) (i.e. *sensus interior*)[1]. Erigena always distinguishes carefully between interior sense and exterior sense, and again between exterior sense and the five senses[2].

---

[1] Mr R. L. Poole renders Erigena's *intellectus, ratio, sensus*, reason, understanding, sense. Obviously there is much to be said for this. On the other hand, there is a great convenience, when translating Erigena's repeated variations upon this theme, in being able to use the adjectives corresponding formally with the nouns, as intellect, intellectual; reason, rational; sense, sensible or sensitive. This decided me for the latter practice.

[2] The term "inner sense" is used by Locke and Kant, but with a meaning

The five senses are like the five gates of a city, and what they admit, exterior sense, like an *ostiarius*, introduces to interior sense (*praesidenti interiori sensui annunciat*)[1]. The five senses are called αἰσθητήρια, *quasi* αἰσθήσεως τήρια, *sensus custodiae*. Exterior sense is called αἴσθησις. It is sense, as distinguished from the senses; it is simplex in its nature, and is seated in the heart. It does not belong to the essence of the soul, but rather to a conjunction of soul and body. But interior sense is διάνοια, the third of the trinity of intellect, reason, and sense, in the soul of man (569). Exterior sense may be deceived, as with a flame and the reflection of it. It is for interior sense to judge of these external impressions (725 B).

Augustine had found a triune character in man, in *esse*, *velle*, *scire*[2]. Dionysius had distinguished another triad in *essentia*, *virtus*, *operatio*[3]. Erigena reconciles these by remarking that there is no *virtus* of humanity more natural or more substantial than to *will* what is right, and that the *operatio* of the rational nature is to *know*, as far as I can know, myself and God (942 A). Augustine had distinguished yet another triad in human nature, as *mens, notitia sui, amor*, or *esse, nosse, amare*[4]. As in the Divine Nature the Spirit proceeds from the Father through the Son, so in the nature of man love proceeds from the mind through self-consciousness (*amor ex mente per notitiam sui procedat*) (610 C).

There are three universal motions of the human spirit— the first is of the soul, the second of reason, the third of sense.

entirely different, viz. that (in Professor Ward's words) "the facts of mind are perceived by an inner sense and the facts of matter by the outer senses." With Erigena *sensus interior* means a sort of faculty of sensibility, of which external sense is the minister, and the five senses the special instruments.

[1] Cf. Augustine, *Conf.* VII. 17.   [2] *Conf.* XIII. 11.
[3] *Coel. Hier.* XI. 2.   [4] *De Civ. Dei*, XI. 26.

The first is a motion around God, and defies definition, for God Himself cannot be defined. It *is* the human intellect. The second motion knows God as the cause of all created things (572 D). It is λόγος or δύναμις, *ratio* or *virtus* (577 A). The third motion knows things in their multiplicity and individuality as visible appearances, as *phantasiae* (573). It is διάνοια or ἐνέργεια, *sensus* or *operatio* (577 D). In other words, what sense knows as separate and multiple in its *operatio*, in actual effects; reason knows as one and simplex in its *virtus*, in the primal causes; and intellect knows ineffably in its *essentia*, in God.

Οὐσία, *essentia*, answers to *intellectus*, and thus God the Father is specially represented in the soul (579 A). Δύναμις, *virtus*, answers to *ratio*, and thus God the Son is specially represented in reason (579 A). Ἐνέργεια, *operatio*, answers to *sensus*, and thus God the Spirit is specially represented in sense (579 A).

It is natural that the triune nature of God should be reflected generally in the creation and specially in man, for man is not merely the climax of creation,—he is both the epitome of creation and the medium of creation.

Man is the microcosm in the strictest sense of the word[1]. He is the summary of all existence. According to Maximus, there are five divisions of being[2], (*a*) the uncreated and the created; (*b*) the intelligible and the sensible; (*c*) heaven and earth (*terra*); (*d*) Paradise and the world (*orbis terrarum*); (*e*) masculine and feminine. Humanity contains in itself all these divisions (530); there is no creature that is not recapi-

---

[1] φασὶ γὰρ μικρὸν εἶναι κόσμον τὸν ἄνθρωπον, ἐκ τῶν αὐτῶν τῷ παντὶ στοιχείων συνεστηκότα. *De Hominis Opificio*, c. xvi (177 D, Vol. 44, ed. Migne).

[2] κατὰ διαδοχὴν διὰ τῶν πρὸ αὐτῶν εἰς αὐτοὺς διαδοθέντα λαβόντες ἅγιοι φασὶ πέντε διαιρέσεσι διειλῆφθαι τὴν πάντων τῶν γεγονότων ὑπόστασιν. *Ambigua* 1304 D, Vol. 91, ed. Migne).

tulated in man. The sensible and the intelligible are the extremes of nature, for there is nothing in the universe lower than body or higher than soul (*intellectus*), as Augustine said: Between God and the mind of man, there is no creature interposed (531).

These divisions are the result of the sin of man. But for the Fall there would have been no separation of the sexes, or of the world and Paradise, or of earth and heaven (536 B). All differences of quality and quantity, of space and time, are also the result of evil (533 B).

Body and Soul. The division of body and soul is not strictly the result of sin, for when man was created in the image of God, soul and body were created together, and the soul therefore precedes the body only in dignity, not in space or in time. But the body as we know it, material and corruptible, came into existence after man's sin, and because of it (582). It was man, after he had transgressed, who made to himself this fragile and mortal body. This is signified by the fig-leaves, which are a shade, excluding the rays of the sun, as our bodies shade our souls in the darkness of ignorance, and exclude the light of truth (583)[1]. God is immortal, and all that He creates is immortal: it is therefore impossible that he should have created our mortal body. But where, then, is that spiritual and incorruptible body which belonged to man before his sin? Being incorruptible, it cannot have perished. It is hidden in the secret recesses (*in secretis sinibus*) of our nature, and it will reappear in the future, when this mortal shall put on immortality (584).

The soul (*anima*) is the image of God, and the body is the image of the soul (585 D). So that our mortal body, since the Fall, has been an image of an image (598 C). This

[1] Cf. Gregory Nazianzen, *Orat.* 39.

thought, borrowed from Gregory of Nyssa[1], continually recurs (790 A).

Human nature is one and simplex, free from all composition and dissimilitude and multiplicity of parts. It is only an absurd simplicity that divides human nature into parts, as if it were a composite of similars and dissimilars. If the Divinity is one and undivided, humanity, as made in the image of the Divinity, must be one and undivided also, and all men, none excepted, are one in it (922 A, C). One man is greater than the whole of the visible universe, because of the dignity of his rational nature. As Augustine says: *Nam si melior est anima vermiculi quam corpus solare totum mundum illustrans* (784 D).

Life. Life is divided into two classes, rational life and irrational life. Rational life belongs to angels and men, but is usually distinguished as intellectual life in angels and rational life in men. Wherever there is intellect or reason, there is the image of God (732). Irrational life is divided into sensible life, as in animals, and senseless life, as in plants. There are thus four species of created life, as there are four elements. Existence, without life, adds a fifth class of being. So that all that exists falls into one or more of these five classes—it is, it lives, it feels, it reasons, it knows (621 B)[2].

All the four species of created life,—intellectual, as in angels; rational, as in men; sensible, as in animals; and senseless, as in plants,—are contained in man, who is rightly called *creaturarum omnium officina*, because he contains

---

[1] ὁ δὲ νοῦς τῷ κατ᾿ εἰκόνα τοῦ καλοῦ γεγενῆσθαι, καὶ αὐτὸς ἔχει τὸ καλὸς εἶναι· ἡ δὲ φύσις ἡ ὑπὸ τοῦ νοῦ συνεχομένη, καθάπερ τις εἰκὼν εἰκόνος ἐστί. Gregory of Nyssa, *De Hominis Opificio*, c. xii (164 A, Vol. 44, ed. Migne).

[2] οὐδέν ἐστι τῶν ὄντων ὃ παντελῶς ἀφῄρηται τὸ ἔχειν τινα δύναμιν· ἀλλ᾿ ἢ νοεράν, ἢ λογικήν, ἢ αἰσθητικήν, ἢ ζωτικήν, ἢ οὐσιώδη δύναμιν ἔχει. *De Div. Nom.* VIII. 3 (892 B, Vol. 3, ed. Migne).

every creature within himself. He knows as an angel, reasons as a man, feels as an animal, lives as a plant. *Intelligit quidem ut angelus, ratiocinatur ut homo, sentit ut animal irrationale, vivit ut germen, corpore animaque subsistit, nullius creaturae expers.* These species of life are not all contained in an angel, for sense is only found in bodies constituted of the four elements. There is no sight where there is not fire; no hearing where there is not air; no touch where there is not earth, and neither smell nor taste where there is not water. But the body of an angel is spiritual and simplex, and lacks all sensible qualities. An angel does not know things phenomenally (*per phantasias corporum*), but perceives them spiritually in their spiritual causes (733 B, C). But even senseless life is represented in man, for those parts of the body which are not penetrated by the air do not participate in sense, and so the bones, the nails, and the hair have only a vegetable life (*vim germinalis vitae aperit*) (734 A).

As the greater number includes the lesser numbers in it, so the creation of man includes the creation of the whole universe (782 D).

Erigena adopts the doctrine of Gregory of Nyssa that humanity is a medium between the two extremes of the incorporeal nature of God, and the irrational life of the animals (795 B). This thought is also elaborated by Maximus, and became one of the central features of Erigena's teaching. As man is the middle point between the extremes of spiritual and corporeal, a unique union of soul and body, it is natural to suppose that every creature, visible and invisible, from one extreme to the other, is created (*condita est*) in man (893 C), and that all are reunited and reconciled in man (534 D).

Man both Animal and Spiritual. The creation of man is narrated twice, first as in the image of God, and second as in the genus of animals (750 B, C). In the first place it is written : *And God said, Let us make man in our image, after our likeness* (Gen. i. 26), and there is no mention of *the dust*, or of *a living soul*. In the second place it is written : *And the Lord God formed man of the dust of the ground, and breathed into his nostrils the breath of life, and man became a living soul* (Gen. ii. 7), where the same phrase is used, *animam viventem*, as was previously used of the beasts. *Factus, inquit, homo in animam viventem. Non dixit, in spiritum vivificantem* (834 A).

All animals are represented in man, and man in all animals. Man is an animal, and he is not an animal ; inasmuch as he has body, and nutritive life, and irrational appetites, he is an animal ; inasmuch as in his higher nature he possesses reason, and intellect, and interior sense, with the memory of Divine and eternal things, he is not an animal (752). So man is both animal and spiritual, as the Apostle says : *The natural man (animalis homo) perceiveth not the things of the Spirit of God* (1 Cor. ii. 14) ; and again : *He that is spiritual (spiritualis homo) judgeth all things* (1 Cor. ii. 15). The animal man is often spoken of in Scripture as *the flesh*, and the spiritual man as *mind, soul*, or *intellect*. It is because of the duplex nature of man that we have the narrative of a twofold creation (753).

The Disciple asks whether man, if he had not sinned, would have been an animal? The Master answers that man, in his first creation in the image of God, was in a sense an animal (*quoddam animal*), a wise and spiritual animal, but when he fell he became unwise, and descended more into the likeness of the brutes (762 A).

It was the will of God to create all creatures, visible and invisible, in man. And if God had not created man in the genus of the animals, or at least if the whole nature of all the animals had not subsisted in man, the universal creature would not have been comprehended in man (764 B).

Thus all the lower creation is in man. But what of the angels? The angels are also in man, in a double sense,— they are coessential with him, as belonging to the same order of intellectual as distinguished from sensible creatures, and by mutual knowledge and reciprocal intellect, man is in the angel and the angel is in man (783 A). When we dispute, in so far as we really understand each other, my mind becomes yours, and your mind becomes mine. So since angels and men reciprocally know each other, the angelic nature becomes one with men, and the human nature becomes one with the angels (780 B, C).

The Disciple objects that this doctrine of the duplex nature of man must mean that there are two souls in man, one which vivifies and administers the body, and one which subsists in reason and intellect, which is an absurd conclusion. The Master replies that the soul is one and simplex, but is called by different names according to the different motions. As it moves around the Divine Essence, it is mind, soul, intellect; as it considers the natural causes of created things, it is reason; as it receives knowledge of sensible things, it is sense; as it nourishes and actuates the body, it is vital motion (*vitalis motus*). But it is one in all, and all in one (754). All creatures are thus summarised and contained in man, for every creature belongs to one of these five classes—it is either corporeal (as a stone) or vital (as a plant) or sensible (as an animal) or rational (as a man) or intellectual (as an angel). *Aut enim corporea est, aut vitalis, aut sensitiva, aut rationalis, aut intellectualis.*

Though man is thus of a double nature, animal and spiritual, he may regain simplicity of nature, for he may become wholly animal (by a life of sin) or wholly spiritual (by a life of holiness). But one is the result of his own free will alone, and the other is the result of his free will and the grace of God together (755).

All that was originally created in man necessarily remains eternally whole and incorrupt. It was not the nature of man that sinned, but a perverse will, which was irrationally moved against the rational nature (760 B, C).

The Image of God in Man. There are two attributes of the soul of man in which we may clearly recognise the image of God. As God is diffused through all things, and yet comprehended by none, so the soul penetrates the body and yet is not enclosed by it. And as we know that God is, while it is impossible to define what He is, so the soul knows that it is, but neither the soul nor any other creature knows what it is (788 A)[1].

The whole nature of man is made in the image of God, though strictly and mainly (*proprie et principaliter*) the image subsists in the soul alone, for the soul derives directly from God, without the interposition of any other creature, and the vital motion derives from the soul, and the body derives from the vital motion (790 D). The vital motion is nothing but a certain conjunction and connection of soul and body, mutually depending upon each other, whereby the body is formed from the soul, for when the body and soul are separated, the vital motion ceases (791).

[1] Cf. Gregory of Nyssa, *De Hominis Opificio*, c. xi (153 D, Vol. 44, ed. Migne).

While the image of God is seen most clearly in the more excellent nature of man, that is to say, in his intelligent nature, with its triune constitution of intellect, reason, and sense (*sensus interior*), yet if we consider the human soul more diligently we shall remember that its nature is *simplicissima*, without any parts which might be regarded as superior or inferior. But while the soul is wholly and everywhere itself, its various motions have various appellations. As contemplating God, it is intellect, mind, soul; as investigating the reasons of natural things, it is reason; as finding, discerning, and defining these, it is interior sense; as receiving images (*phantasiae*) of these by means of corporeal organs, it is exterior sense; and as administering the body in growth and nutrition, it is vital motion. Yet all the time it is a most simplex and individual and incommunicable essence (787).

The interior nature of man is triune, for it consists of the soul, which rules all that is below itself, and contemplates that which is above itself, that is, the Divine Nature; and reason, which seeks to investigate the grounds of all things that can be known or felt; and interior sense, which receives, discerns, and judges the impressions (*phantasiae*) presented by the bodily senses (325 B).

The exterior nature of man is also triune, for it comprises sense, and the vital motion, and the material body (825 A). So that human nature is sixfold; it exists, and lives, and feels through the body, and feels apart from the body, and reasons, and knows. *Est enim, et vivit, et sentit per corpus, sentit extra corpus, ratiocinatur, intelligit* (825 B).

As at one extreme of human nature, beyond the soul there is only God, so at the other extreme, beneath the body there is only nothing—not the *nihil* which is so called because of the excellence of its nature (because it is superessential) but the *nihil* which is the total privation of being. *Siquidem ultra animum solus Deus est, infra materiam, corpus dico solum, nihil est; non illud nihil, quod per excellentiam naturae, sed illud, quod per privationem totius naturae et dicitur et cogitatur* (825 C).

Man is a thought eternally created in the mind of God. *Homo est notio quaedam intellectualis in mente divina aeternaliter facta.* To define man as an animal, as rational, as mortal, and so forth, is to define him not by what he essentially is, but by the accidents which result from generation. But the notion of man in the mind of God is nothing like these: it surpasses all definition.

Knowledge and Reality. The notion of things, as created in the human mind, is the actual substance of the things, as the notion of the universe in the mind of God is the incommunicable substance of the universe (769 A). All visible and invisible creatures are created in man alone, for no substance is created which is not understood in him. All species, differences, properties, accidents, which are found in natural things, are either naturally contained in him, or are in his knowledge (772 D). And that knowledge is better than the things of which it is the knowledge, inasmuch as the nature is better in which the knowledge is found. The things exist more truly, that is to say, in the notions of man than they exist in themselves (774 A).

As all things subsist *causaliter* in the mind of God, so all things subsist *effectualiter* in human knowledge (*in humana cognitione*) (779 C). Sensible things are made for the sake of (*propter*) sense, not sense for the sake of sensible things (785 A).

How then does man receive his knowledge of the world—

which is a sort of secondary creation of the world, since all exists *causaliter* in the knowledge of God and *effectualiter* in the knowledge of man—before time, as created in the primal causes, or in time, as existing by generation? In both ways,—in the first, as knowing causes; in the second, as knowing effects (776 D).

If man had not sinned, he would not have been among the parts of the world, and he would have known and ruled all things by intellectual understanding of them in their interior causes. But when man fell, he fell from the unity and dignity of his nature, and, for his punishment, took his place among the ignoble parts of the world (782 C).

The body, as first created, is spiritual and immortal, and such it will be again after the Resurrection (800 B). Whatever in the body is immutable, belongs to the first creation; whatever is variable is an addition to its first nature. One and the same form is found in all human bodies, and it remains always immutable in all (801 C). The numberless differences between men are accidents of the form, which do not belong to the original creation, but to the corruptible qualities of generated nature. The spiritual form is, in fact, the spiritual body, which was made in the first creation.

All that is here compounded from the substance of the world will necessarily be resolved into the substance of the world again. The material body will be dissolved into the elements of which it is composed (802 B). The material body is superadded because of sin, and it is not so much a true body, as a kind of changeable and corruptible vestment of the spiritual body (803 A).

Was the body of man mortal, as first created? Erigena answers by quoting Augustine to the effect that as our flesh is vulnerable, though it may never be wounded, so the body of man, as it was created, was mortal, though it need not necessarily have died (804 A)[1].

Erigena contradicts himself upon this point, for he says expressly elsewhere that all that God creates is immortal, as He Himself is immortal, and that the spiritual body which belonged to man before his sin was incorruptible and imperishable (584 A, C). In still another place he declares that God created the whole nature of man, body and soul, alike immortal and incorruptible (884 C, D).

Where is the life of the body at the time of the dissolution of the body? When the body was compounded, it was not compounded, and when the body is dissolved it is not dissolved (729 B). The soul, being spiritual, is nearer in nature to those elements into which the body is dissolved (inasmuch as they are simplex, incorporeal and invisible, and therefore approach the spiritual nature) than to the corporeality of the body (730 A). What wonder, then, if the soul continues to rule (*agat*), though not in any corporeal sense, the different parts of the body, when it is dissolved into the elements? (732 B).

When any part of the body is corrupted from its natural integrity, the soul does not manifest itself there; not that the soul is defective, but that the corrupted part is unable to receive the virtue of the soul (793 B).

The Fall of Man. The source of all such corruption, and of all the evil in human nature, is the Fall, the Scriptural account of which is expounded as allegorical throughout. Only the briefest time, or none at all, elapsed between the Creation and the Fall. If man spent some time in Paradise, and was nourished on the Tree of Life, why had he not a happy progeny there? (810 C). And how would it be said that

[1] *De Baptismo*, I.

the Devil *was a murderer from the beginning* (John viii. 44) if there was a temporal space in which he was not a murderer, and in which man had not sinned? Yet man fell first in himself, before he was tempted of the Devil (811 C).

Erigena gives, at great length, a mystical interpretation of all the details in the story of the Fall, mainly derived from Gregory of Nyssa and Ambrose. Everything is spiritualised.

Thus Paradise is not a place but a state. Origen held that there is no other Paradise than the third heaven, into which the Apostle Paul was caught up. Manifestly, then, Paradise is spiritual and not local (*spiritualem profecto et illocalem*) (861 B, C) (818 C). Paradise is human nature in its first state, as created in the image of God (822 A). The four rivers are the four cardinal virtues (816 B). The serpent is delight (*delectatio*); the man, mind; the woman, sense (815 C)[1]. For falsity belongs to corporeal sense. No other part of human nature receives falsity, in the first instance, but exterior sense. It is through it that interior sense and reason and intellect are deceived (826 B). Some of the senses are like an extension of the body, as the heel is the bodily extremity, and so it is said: *Et tu insidiaberis calcaneo ejus* (Gen. iii. 15), for it is in these bodily senses that evil lies in wait for us (854 A, C). The sleep of Adam is the turning away of the soul, which ought always to have been inflexibly fixed upon the contemplation of the Creator, to the delights of material things and carnal appetites (835 D). The order of the Divine Law is that the Creator should be known first in His ineffable beauty, and then the creature, and that all the beauty of the creature (whether internal, in its reasons, or external, in its sensible forms) should be referred to the

[1] Cf. Augustine, *De Trin.* XII. 13.

praise of God. But man, proudly spurning the Law of God, preferred the knowledge and the love of the material creature to the Creator (843 C).

The serpent is *in* the woman: it is carnal concupiscence, and delight in corporeal things, arising from an irrational motion of the soul (847 C). Neither the man nor the woman is cursed, but the serpent alone. God does not curse, but blesses, what He has made, and man and woman, that is, soul and sense, are creatures of God. But carnal delight receives the severe sentence, because it is beyond the creation of God: it was not in the nature which God made (848 C). The fig-leaves signify the letter of the Divine Law as against the spirit of it; the perverse and corrupt use and understanding of the Law of God as against the true and spiritual use and understanding of it (839 A). The expulsion from Paradise is the loss of that natural felicity which man possessed when he was created. It was not his nature that he lost, for that, as made in the likeness of God, is necessarily incorruptible. He lost the happiness that would have been his, if he had remained obedient to God (863 B). What is said in praise of the life of man in Paradise is said rather by way of reference to the future, if he had been obedient, than to the present, which was merely beginning, and did not last (809 B). If man had remained in Paradise, that is, if human nature had retained its integrity, it would not have suffered the severance into sexes[1], in the likeness of irrational animals, but man would have multiplied in an angelic fashion (836 A)[2]. The sexual division is in the soul, as well as in the

---

[1] It is certainly an exaggeration to say, as Baur does, that Erigena held the separation of the sexes to be "die wichtigste Folge des Falls" (*Lehre der Dreieinigkeit*, II. p. 302). He treats it rather as the most evident example, in the life of humanity, of the divisive force of sin.

[2] Cf. Augustine, *De Genesi*, X. 3. 6.

body, for νοῦς, intellect, is the masculine in the soul, and αἴσθησις, sense, is the feminine (541 A). And the man must rule the woman—soul must rule sense, as it will do in the restored life (855 D).

By the prescience of God, the consequences of sin were created in man and with man before he had sinned, since with God there is no before or after (808 A),—a statement which is inconsistent in itself, and also inconsistent with the whole doctrine of Erigena.

Evil. As goodness is creative, so evil is destructive, in its very nature. If it were possible for evil finally to triumph, all would perish, and evil would perish along with all else (511 A)[1]. For evil is parasitic: it only exists in dependence upon the good.

What is the cause of evil? If it be referred to Nature, it must be further referred to the Creator of Nature. Similarly if the cause of evil be thought to be in the freedom of the will, it must be thought to be ultimately in God, Who made the will of man free. So that the cause of the fault is neither Nature nor free will (974), for in no way can what is good become a cause of evil, and all things that God has created are good. The cause of evil, in so far as it may be said to have a cause, is the irrational motion of the free will, and this cannot be properly referred to the free will, for the irrational motion is not properly relative to the free will, but contrary to it. It is an abuse of good: it is a good used evilly (975). Let who will seek the cause of this abuse and this perversity: none can be found. In this sense, evil is causeless. It is foolish to seek the cause of that which is not contained in any genus, or any species, or in the number of the good things created by the Highest Goodness, for

[1] Cf. Augustine, *Conf.* VII. 12; *De Civ. Dei*, XIX. 13.

all that the Creator did not make is wholly causeless and substanceless (*penitus incausale et insubstantiale*) (976) (944).

There is nothing vicious in any rational creature which is not good in some irrational creature. Ferocity is good in a lion, and filth in a pig, for these things are natural to these animals, but in angels and in men, they are vices (967 B, C). No creature is evil, nor is the knowledge of any creature evil. It is the perverse motion of the rational soul, which leaves the Creator, and turns itself to the lustful love of material things, which is evil (844 D). No nature is evil in itself. The nature of the demons is not evil, for as to their essence, they participate in goodness, or they could not exist at all. (That is, they were made by the Divine Goodness, and they were made good, and their existence, their nature, as derived from God, cannot be otherwise than good.) They are evil, not as what they are, but as what they are not. For this doctrine Erigena quotes Dionysius[1]. The nature of the Devil is not evil, for it was created by God. Erigena here quotes a passage from Augustine[2], in which two texts from the Septuagint and Vulgate are applied to the creation of the Evil One : *Hoc est initium figmenti Domini quod fecit, ut illudatur ab angelis ejus* (Job xl. 14)[3], and *Draco hic, quem finxisti ad illudendum ei* (Psalm civ. 26) (927 C, D). It is not the nature or the substance of the Devil that is evil[4], and that will be finally destroyed (for nothing that is from God can be evil or can be destroyed), but his

---

[1] *De Div. Nom.* IV.

[2] *Exemeron*, XI. The passages are quoted in the same connection in *De Civ. Dei*, XI. 15. Origen also (*De Princ.* I. 5) refers Job xl. 14 to the Devil. The LXX reading is : τουτέστιν ἀρχὴ πλάσματος Κυρίου· πεποιημένον ἐγκαταπαίζεσθαι ὑπὸ τῶν ἀγγέλων αὐτοῦ. (It is Job xl. 19 in the English versions.)

[3] See Note in Appendix, p. 197.

[4] Augustine, *De Civ. Dei*, XIX. 13.

hostile will (*voluntas inimica*) which God did not make, but which proceeded from himself (930 C). For this last, Erigena appeals to the authority of Origen[1].

Evil is no more in human nature than it is in the angelic nature. It is not planted in the *nature* of man at all, but it is solely in a perverse motion of the will. *Non ergo in natura humana plantatum est malum, sed in perverso et irrationabili motu rationabilis liberaeque voluntatis est constitutum* (828 D). *Non enim peccata naturalia sunt, sed voluntaria* (944 A). Evil is always seen as good. It is a false good : it is evil hidden under the appearance of good. In itself it is such a deformity that if it were seen aright, it would be fled and abhorred (826 B, C).

The End of Evil. Erigena quotes Gregory of Nyssa for the doctrine that evil cannot be perpetual, but must, in the nature of things, come to an end (*ad certum terminum*) and cease to be (*et quandoque desituram*). For if the Divine Goodness, which always works good (not only in the good, but also in the evil) is infinite and eternal, then necessarily its contrary cannot be infinite and eternal.

Evil will therefore reach its consummation, and will not remain in any nature. For as the shadow of the earth, which is called night, is not extended infinitely into space, but reaches its apex at the distance of a hundred and twenty-six thousand stadia, beyond which the solar rays are diffused around it, so evil, which like a huge shadow, darkens our life, shall be confined by the abundance of the eternal Goodness, and then altogether abolished (*et omnino abolebitur*)

---

[1] *Destrui novissimus inimicus ita intelligendus est, non ut substantia ejus, quae a Deo est, pereat, sed ut voluntas inimica, quae non a Deo sed ab ipso processit, intereat. Destruetur ergo non ut non sit, sed ut inimicus non sit et mors. Nihil enim Omnipotenti impossibile est, insanabile est aliquid Factori suo.* De Princ. III. 6. 5.

(918). Erigena owes this magnificent metaphor to Gregory of Nyssa[1].

What is deformity in a part of the universe, is beauty in the whole[2]. True reason does not tremble to declare that what is evil, misery, retribution, as we see it partially, is not evil, not misery, not retribution, as it is seen in the whole creation (954 A). The dark shadow in the picture, as Augustine has said, contributes to the beauty of the whole painting (953 D)[3].

As it has been said that evil is not in the whole of things, so it cannot really be in the parts of the universe, though it seems to be, and is seen as something illicit, which must be restrained and purged. *Quod enim, ut diximus, in toto malum non est, malum fieri in parte non potest, quamvis videatur esse illicitum, atque purgandum seu refraenandum.*

Nothing is left, therefore, to lessen or to mar the fulness and the beauty of the whole universe, whether here, while this sensible world fulfils its course, or there, when it has returned into its causes, to rest in them for ever (967).

Grace. The optimist theory of Erigena is worked out by means of his doctrine of grace. This is involved in the distinction (of which he makes repeated use) between the *datum* and the *donum* of the Divine Goodness, the distinction being based upon the passage : *Every good gift (datum) and every perfect boon (donum) is from above, coming down from the Father of Lights* (James i. 17).

The main distinction between the two is that *esse* is the *datum* and *bene esse* the *donum*. Of Nature we must say : *datur*; of Grace *donatur*; *dationes* are the distributions by

---

[1] Gregory of Nyssa, *De Hominis Opificio*, c. xxi (201 C–204 A, Vol. 44, ed. Migne).

[2] Cf. Augustine, *Conf.* VII. 13.   [3] *De Civ. Dei*, XI. 23.

which all Nature subsists; *donationes* are the distributions of grace, by which all subsisting Nature is adorned. There are two modes of *bene esse*, one in which all things are said to be good, as created by the goodness of God; the other in which the gift of virtue is added, and the natural goodness becomes more apparent as being adorned by virtue. No nature whatever is without participation in the Divine Grace. As all participate in goodness, in so far as they are, so all participate in grace, in so far as they are beautiful as well as good (631).

The *datum* is the subsistence of the universe, from the intellectual nature, which is the highest, to the corporeal, which is the lowest[1]. The goodness of God does not only give (*dat*) all things to be, but also to be eternally. No essence or substance is created by God which does not eternally and incommunicably remain (903).

But between *esse* and *aeternaliter esse* there is a certain medium (*medietas quaedam*) which is *bene esse*, without which the extremes of *esse* and *semper esse* are not truly, though they are (*nec vere sunt, quamvis sint, nec recte dicuntur esse*), for *esse* and *semper esse*, without *bene esse*, is neither *vere esse*, nor *vere semper esse*. That alone truly is, and truly always is, which subsists in goodness and in blessedness (*illud enim vere et est et semper est, quod bene ac beate subsistit*).

This *bene esse* is the *donum* of God. It is effected by the free will of the creature and that *donum* which the Scriptures call Grace. This *bene esse* is not universally given, but only to angels and men; to intellectual and rational natures; and not universally to these, but only to the angels who kept their first estate and to men who are elect (904 A).

[1] *Coel. Hier.* IV. 2.

Briefly, nature is the *datum*; grace is the *donum*. Nature brings the non-existent into existence. Grace brings some of the existent, beyond all existence, into union with God. It is the *datum* which gives the substantial existence of the universal creature; it is the *donum* that gives the final deification of the elect (905 A).

Upon the distinction between the *datum* and the *donum* largely depends also Erigena's doctrine of retribution.

Retribution. The future punishment of the wicked is spiritual. The fire, the worm, the gnashing of teeth, the lake of brimstone, are not to be understood as corporeal and local. For this Erigena quotes Ambrose[1]. The forms of retribution are not to be understood as existing in any part of the creature, or of the universe, as created by God, but as solely in the perverse motion of the evil will, and the corrupt conscience, and in late and fruitless remorse. As faith without works is dead, so is sin without the possibility of sinning, and evil without the possibility of evildoing. The evil desire remains, without what it desires, and so the flame of sinful desire cannot burn in anything but itself (936 A, B).

Where is Judas tormented, but in his polluted conscience, who betrayed his Lord? What punishment does he suffer but his belated and useless repentance, which burns like a flame for ever? What does Dives suffer in hell, but the privation of those splendid banquets which he enjoyed in this life? What flame consumes the wicked king Herod, but his own fury, which murdered the innocents? (937 A, B).

The Disciple is now persuaded, by what has been quoted from Ambrose, that future punishment will not be corporeal, sensible, local, or temporal. How can it be, when after the

---

[1] *Expos. in Lucam*, especially on c. xiii and xiv.

consummation of all things, there exist no longer sensible
bodies, or space, or time? (938 B, D). Future retribution must
be like future blessedness, eternal, and not understood in
any spatial or temporal sense. But though now persuaded
that the future torment of the wicked will be spiritual, the
Disciple still wants to know in what it will be found? The
Master answers that only three answers are possible. What
is punished must be either what absolutely does not exist
in Nature (which is absurd, for nothing can be punished
which does not somehow exist); or some natural subsistence
(which is equally contrary to reason, for every natural subsistence depends upon God for its existence, and cannot be
punished); or *what is not*, and yet is punished in some
existing subject, the subject itself being free from punishment (940 B, C).

The Evil Will. There is no other seat of punishment, as
there is no other seat of corruption, but the perverse motion
of the will, which is neither from God, nor from created
Nature, but is causeless, for it is nothing but a privation and
a defect of the natural will (959 C). Punishment, like sin, is
not of the nature, but of the will.

The evil will—the irrational motion of it—is punished in
beings whose nature is good, rational, and impassible. And
as the evil will does not contaminate the natural good—the
nature which, as created by God, is good, and cannot be
anything but good—so the torment of the evil will does not
torment the natural subject to which it is attached and in
which it is contained (943 C). So, what is itself incapable of
punishment sustains by its virtue, and allows to be punished,
that which is punished (960 A).

The illicit will of evil angels and evil men is tormented in
themselves, in their memories, because what they desired in

this life, and wished in the future, they will not find (944 D). The punishment is by way of *phantasiae*[1]—which are not to be understood as altogether unreal (*non esse*), because they are images in the memory of natural forms (959 D). The Disciple asks how these phantasies differ from falsities? The Master answers that what is false merely is not. A fable, such as that of Daedalus, is false. But a *phantasia* is a kind of image and appearance of something, whether visible or invisible, impressed upon the memory, though the reality is not as it is thought of in the image (962 B, C). There can be no *phantasia* of what does not exist in Nature (963 A). (It is in fact a perverted thought or a perverted desire, which goes back to something which did exist in the universe.)

The reward of the righteous, like the retribution of the wicked, consists in *phantasiae*, but in the case of the righteous these are properly called theophanies. The righteous will see God in more and more intimate manifestations, that is, but God is, and ever will be, invisible in Himself. *He dwells in unapproachable light* (1 Tim. vi. 16) (919 C) (963 C). That other word of the Apostle, *Now we see in a mirror darkly, but then face to face* (1 Cor. xiii. 12), means that the redeemed will see the nearest theophany—as much as is comprehensible to a creature of the incomprehensible cause of all (926 C).

The human nature of the righteous and of the unrighteous alike is saved (*salva*) and whole (*integra*) and uncontaminated. In both alike the spiritual body is free from all

---

[1] Erigena's conception of *phantasiae* is borrowed from Augustine. "Phantasms are nothing else than figments drawn by the bodily senses from bodily forms; which, to commit to memory, as they have been received, to divide, multiply, contract, enlarge, order, disarrange, or in any other way image in the mind by thinking, is very easy; but to avoid and escape, where truth is sought, difficult." (*De vera Relig.* 10.)

animality and corruption, and of like glory of nature, of like essence, and of like eternity.

The distance between the saved and the lost is not a distance of space, but the distance which exists between happiness and misery. Peter and Judas were both present at the Last Supper and both locally near to Christ, but really and spiritually the one was near to Him and the other far from Him (983 C, D). Nearness is likeness, and distance is unlikeness. It is not the strides of the body, but the affections of the mind that take us far from God, and that bring us near to Him (871 D). It is not mass or space which separates Paradise and the world, but diversity of intercourse and difference of beatitude (*sed diversitate conversationis, differentiaque beatitudinis*) (538 B).

An incomparably greater number will be brought to life by the passion of Christ than were brought to death by the transgression of Adam, for *where sin abounded, grace did much more abound* (Rom. v. 20) (1007 C).

The Last Judgment. When we say, *Inde venturus judicare vivos et mortuos*, we are not to think of the Last Judgment as a sensible scene, but as a judgment which takes place in each man's conscience, where within himself the books shall be opened, and God shall reveal the hidden things of darkness, and every man shall be the judge of his own actions and thoughts (*et unusquisque suarum actionum et cogitationum judex erit*) (997 B).

The corporeal images used of future punishment in the Scriptures and in the Fathers are used for the sake of the simple faithful (986 D). They are figurative, as Ambrose attests (971 B). It is absurd to think of hell as a place under the earth (954 C), for the earth shall altogether perish. How can a place remain when there is nothing local, or a time when there is nothing temporal? This is the sufficient reason why future torment cannot be sensible or corporeal (971 A).

The *drop of cold water* in the Parable of Dives and Lazarus means the distribution of the merits of the Saints, for even the disembodied may ask the help of the Saints, whether to be wholly delivered from their misery, or that they may be less tormented (977 A, B). This is noticeable as being one of the surprisingly few theological details in which we are reminded that our philosopher was a mediaeval Catholic.

Though hell is not in the nature of things, it is amongst that which returns to God (964 D), in this sense, that He contains all, for darkness is contained in light, and silence in sound, and shadow in body. The causes of those things which are contraries are constituted in the things of which they are contraries (965 A). The occasion of darkness resides in light, for darkness is the privation of light, and there cannot be the privation of anything unless the thing itself exists (552 C). If light did not precede, the absence of it, which is darkness, would not follow. Every absence has its cause of birth from that of which it is the absence. The thing itself, and the absence of it, are of one genus, as light and darkness; sound and silence; form and formlessness (943 A).

In spite of all his minimising tendencies in this region Erigena strives to retain orthodox doctrine by some positive and emphatic statements as to retribution. Thus, he says that hell is *quiddam lugubre lacrimabileque, gravemque desperationis plenum inevitabilemque carcerem, omniumque bonorum egestatem in phantasticis vanissimisque visionibus* (971 C).

The **Restoration of All Things**. The restoration of all things, ἡ ἀποκατάστασις πάντων (Acts iii. 21), which Erigena consistently calls *adunatio*, is already begun in humanity. It began with the Resurrection of Christ, for in the Risen Christ there was neither male nor female[1]. The division into sexes (like all other divisions in human nature) is the result of sin, for if man had not fallen, his nature would have remained simplex. Humanity is restored to its first simplicity of nature in Christ (532 B, D). Every division is united again in Him. Not only male and female, the lowest of the five divisions of Maximus, but all the other divisions disappear in Christ, for when risen, He was at once in Paradise and in the world, in heaven and on earth (538 C), and since His humanity became absolutely one with His divinity, the divisions of the sensible and the intelligible, and of the created and the uncreated, were also resolved in Him[2]. Since the humanity of the Risen Lord was changed into the divinity (*translata est in divinitatem*) it transcends space and time, quality and quantity, and all circumscribed form (*forma circumscripta*). This is true of the whole humanity of Christ, *corpus, anima, intellectus*, and to this same unity and glory He will bring His elect, after the General Resurrection, when they will be one with Him and in Him (539).

Body, sense, soul, and intellect are the four parts which constitute human nature. All these Christ assumed, and united (*adunavit*) in Himself, so that He was the perfect man. After the Resurrection these were not four in Him, but one, *et non compositum unum, sed simpliciter unum corpus et sensus, anima et intellectus*. All creatures, therefore, are united and redeemed in Him, for in man, in the totality of his

[1] Cf. Maximus, *Expos. Orat. Dom.* (890 D, Vol. 90, ed. Migne).
[2] Cf. Maximus, *Mystagogia* (667 B, Vol. 91, ed. Migne).

humanity, every creature is represented. All creatures are either sensible or intelligible, and both these divisions of created life are found in man, and were assumed by Christ (541).

The image of God is neither masculine nor feminine (896 B). The division of the sexes is one result of sin. The reunion began in Christ after the Resurrection, though He still appeared to His Disciples in the virile form with which they were familiar, since they could not have recognised Him otherwise (894 A) (538 A).

The humanity of the Risen Christ is made one with the Deity[1]. All is God, and all is man, in the Risen Christ, and all is freed from the bonds of space and time. After the Resurrection He was in Paradise, though He was spiritually manifested to His Disciples upon earth (894 B, D). He is seated on the right hand of the Father, a place which no creature can attain (894 C). The right hand of God means the power of God. The heavenly session of Christ is not corporeal and local, but mystical and spiritual (592 B).

What was accomplished in Christ, specially, after His Resurrection, shall be accomplished in all humanity, generally, in the General Resurrection (895 C).

The restoration of humanity in Christ is twofold. All humanity is restored in Him to its pristine condition, but for the elect there is also beatitude and deification, for they ascend unto God. It is one thing to return to Paradise, which is human nature as first created, and another thing to eat of the Tree of Life, which is Christ. Thus the Apostle says: *We shall all rise again, but we shall not all be changed (Omnes quidem resurgemus, sed non omnes immutabimur)* (I Cor.

---

[1] Cf. Augustine, *De Trin.* I. 5.

xv. 51)[1]. As if it were said: We all, no man excepted, shall return to the integrity of our nature as first created, rising in spiritual bodies, but we shall not all be changed into the glory of deification (979 A, B).

The Resurrection. Erigena had thought that the General Resurrection and the restitution of man was solely by the grace of the Redeemer, but his study of Epiphanius and Gregory of Nyssa had convinced him, he tells us, that the resurrection of the dead was *naturali virtute*. He quotes from the former writer a passage, in which the setting and rising of the sun, the death of the seed and the life of the plant, the legend of the phoenix, and so forth, are all treated as natural exemplars of the resurrection (899 B, C). It is the conclusion of Erigena that the natural and vital *virtus*, which never deserts the substance of the human body, itself suffices to restore the body to life, and the whole of human nature to its integrity (900 D). Yet he says, inconsistently, that both nature and grace cooperate in the resurrection (902 D), and again that the resurrection is effected both by the *datum* of natural power and by the *donum* of supernatural grace (904 C).

In the individual death is the starting point of the *adunatio*. The dissolution of the body is the end of man's ruin, for

---

[1] This is the reading of the Vulgate. Erigena remarks that many, nearly all, read the passage thus, but some read it: *We shall all sleep, but we shall not all be changed*, and others, with Chrysostom and Augustine, *We shall all be changed, but we shall not all sleep*. He goes on to say that the latter rendering would mean that all will be changed from the corruptible to the incorruptible and from the mortal to the immortal, while some will not sleep because they will be alive at our Lord's coming. This sense, also, remarks Erigena, is agreeable to the Catholic faith. (980 B, C.)

These various readings are discussed by Augustine more than once: *De Civ. Dei*, xx. 20, *Ad tertiam Quaest. Dulcitii*. Maximus also refers to them, *Quaestiones*, 843 C.

then the return to God begins. So that the death of the flesh might be better called the death of death.

It cannot be thought that God made at once a part, the soul, immortal and incorruptible, and a part, the body, mortal and corruptible. He created the whole nature of man, body and soul, alike immortal and incorruptible. But, because of sin, man had an earthly body (and fallen angels an ethereal body) superadded. This, though superadded to our original nature, was assumed by Christ, when He emptied Himself, and took the form of a servant, and therefore, in the end, the earthly body will be changed into spirit, and the whole man shall be reunited (*adunabitur*) when death shall be swallowed up in victory (884 C, D).

Why should it seem incredible that our earthly bodies should be changed into spirit? They are constituted of incorporeal qualities, and why should not that which is constituted by the incorporeal return into the incorporeal? We see in this world how clouds vanish into air, and air into light (885 A, B). So the earthly, mortal, changeable mass of the body, compounded of the diverse qualities of the sensible elements, will be dissolved and changed into stable and substantial spirit, which knows not how to change or die (884 B).

The Stages of Restoration. Five stages may be distinguished in the return of human nature to God: (*a*) The dissolution of the material body into the four elements, (*b*) The Resurrection, when each will receive his body again, restored from the elements, (*c*) The change of the body into spirit, (*d*) The return of the spirit (and of the whole of human nature which has now become spirit) into the primal causes, (*e*) The passage of the spiritualised nature, with its causes, into God, when all shall be in God, as the air is in the sunlight, and appears to be indistinguishable from it, though the air is one thing, and the light another. So shall God be all in all, when there shall be nothing but God (*quando nihil erit nisi solus Deus*).

This does not mean that the substance of anything will perish, but that it will return into what is higher. The passage of human nature into God is not a destruction of substance, but a wonderful and ineffable reversion to its first state, lost by the Fall. If we become one with that which we understand, what wonder if we become one with God, when we see Him face to face? (876 A, B).

The Disciple asks if the restoration of all things means that animals and trees are to be restored? The Master answers that all things, as created in man, are restored in the resurrection of man, not in their corporeal mass and natural species, but in their causes and grounds (*rationes*) (913 B, D), in which indeed they exist more truly than in corporeal and sensible effects. For what exists in time and space and sense has not a real and substantial existence but is a kind of image of real existence. It is like an echo or a shadow, with no independent existence of its own (914 A).

The substance of the corporeal is intelligible, for matter is constituted by the concourse of immaterial and intelligible qualities (885 A, B). There is thus nothing incredible in intelligible substances being united, each not ceasing to possess its own property and subsistence, the inferior being always contained in the superior. When what is lower is attracted and absorbed by what is higher, the lower does not cease to be, but it subsists more worthily in the higher. The air does not lose its substance when it becomes radiant with the sunlight so that nothing can be seen but light;

nor the iron when it becomes incandescent in the fire, so
that nothing can be seen but fire. So the body does not
lose its substance in becoming one with the soul, nor the
soul in becoming one with God (879 A, B). These images of
the sunny air and the glowing iron are borrowed immediately from Maximus, but they were used before his time[1].
Erigena recurs to them often, and once calls them *pulcher-
rima paradigmata* (451 A).

In the *adunatio*, the inferior in each case passes into the
superior, until at last all is reunited with God, and is one in
Him. Yet there is no confusion and no destruction of
essence or substance (893 D). There are many examples
already present in the world of such union of natures
without confusion or composition, as many genera are in
one essence (οὐσία) and many species in one genus; all
numbers in the monad; all lines in the point (881 C, D).

So many may be one, without ceasing to be many.
Many people may see one thing, and see it all at once,
as when a crowd is watching the golden ball on a spire, and
no one says, Take away your glance, so that I may see
what you see! for all can see it together. Many lamps in a
church give one light[2]. Many sounds make one harmony
(883 A, D).

The return of all things to God is the accomplishment of
a vast cycle, smaller analogies of which abound in the
world. The words: *Let the earth bring forth the living
creature after its kind* (*in genere suo*), *cattle and creeping
thing and beast of the earth after its kind* (*secundum species*

---

[1] ὡς ἀὴρ δὲ ὅλου πεφωτισμένος φωτὶ καὶ πυρὶ σίδηρος, ὅλος ὅλῳ πεπυρακτωμένος,
ἢ εἴ τι ἄλλο τῶν τοιούτων ἐστίν. *Ambigua*, 1075 A. The first metaphor is also
found in Augustine, *De Civ. Dei*, XI. 10, and the second in Origen, *De Princ.*
II. 6.

[2] This metaphor is from Dionysius, *De Div. Nom.* II. 4.

suas) (Gen. i. 24) show that the art of Dialectic which divides genera into species, and resolves species into genera, is not merely a human device, but is created in the nature of things, and by the Author of all arts that are true arts (749 D) (705 A). So that man is not the maker of any true art, but the discoverer of it. *Non enim intellectus naturalium artium factor est, sed inventor, non tamen extra se, sed intra eas invenit* (658 B). Now all the arts fulfil a cycle, and illustrate the principle by which all created things return to God. Thus Dialectic begins with οὐσία, descends through genera and species, and returns to οὐσία. Arithmetic begins with the monad and ends with it. Geometry begins with the point (σημεῖον, *signum*) and proceeds through lines, surfaces, angles, length, breadth, and so forth, finally resolving all once more into the point. Music begins with the tone and proceeds through symphonies, simple or composite, and resolves all again into the tone. Astrology begins with the atom (*ab atomo*) and resolves all into it again. Hereupon the Disciple enquires why Grammar and Rhetoric are left out of this list of arts? The Master answers that it is for a double reason; first because many philosophers, not without reason, account them branches of Dialectic, which is the mother of arts[1], and second, because

---

[1] Hauréau has completely misunderstood and misrepresented Erigena upon this point. "Jean Scot...ne voyant dans la dialectique enseignée de son temps qu'un appendice à la grammaire, la méprisa comme une science vaine, et, du premier saut, il voulut se transporter dans une autre région; mais il s'y égara. On ne suivit pas ce perilleux exemple, et, comme il était nécessaire de prouver que Jean Scot, en dédaignant la dialectique, l'avait calomniée, on substitua peu à peu dans l'exposition des thèses logiques, les choses aux mots, les affirmations aux simples conjectures. Ainsi la dialectique se confondit avec la métaphysique. Il ne s'agissait, pour opérer confusion, que d'admettre comme vraie toute proposition démontrée suivant les règles. Or, dans l'état de la science et dans l'état des âmes, également portées à tout croire par leur ignorance et par leur super-

they do not belong so much to the region of natural things as to that of human speech (869), which was Aristotle's opinion (*Aristoteles cum suis sectatoribus approbat*). But the principle of return is true of these arts also, for they begin with letters and hypotheses, and resolve all into these again (870 A).

The celestial spheres, the sun, the moon, the planets, fulfil their appointed cycles and return to the same place. The sea ebbs and flows. The seasons follow each other and return again. Animals and plants fulfil their lives, and reproduce themselves, and so generation follows generation. And the end of each cycle is the beginning of it, to which it returns, and in which it rests (866). So in the larger process of the world the primal causes descend into the elements, and the elements into bodies; then bodies are resolved into the elements again, and the elements into the primal causes (696 B).

The world reverts into its causes because all things naturally yearn toward their cause, which is God, that they may return to Him, and rest. All things, issuing from their source, degenerate (*vilescerent*), and perish if they cannot return. There is a natural necessity that our mortal bodies should pass, not only into spiritual bodies, but into our souls, for as the soul reverts to its cause, which is God, since it was made in His image, so the body reverts to its cause, which is the soul, since the body is an image of the

---

stitieuse dévotion, on voyait à peine un intervalle là où nous savons aujourd'hui qu'il existe un abîme. La logique étant donc acceptée comme l'art de connaître, on compta bientôt parmi les sophistes, c'est-à-dire parmi les logiciens, ce Jean Scot lui-même, *sanctus sophista Joannes*, qui avait fait profession, dans les termes les plus injurieux, de mépriser la dialectique" (*Histoire de la Philosophie scolastique*, I. pp. 44-45). Fancy the Scot, whose system is as essentially dialectical as that of Hegel, despising dialectic!

soul—*imago imaginis*—and thence to God, Who is the Cause of all (952 C, D).

There is a similar reason why we, who are composite in this life, return to simple unity in the restoration. We are made in the image of the Trinity, which is simplex, inseparable and incomposite, and so, in reverting to our cause, we return to unity and simplicity (953 A).

There is thus a threefold restoration, first, of the sensible world into its causes, by the medium of life; second, of human nature in general, as redeemed in Christ, to its pristine state ; third, of the elect in Christ, into union with God, so that they shall be one with Him and in Him (1020).

The word *deificatio*, Erigena remarks, is rarely used by the Latin Fathers, but the sense of it is found in many of them, and most of all in Ambrose (1015 C).

The Return of the Soul to God. In the whole process of return seven stages are to be distinguished: 1. The earthly body passes into vital motion, 2. The vital motion into sense, 3. Sense into reason, 4. Reason into soul (these five—body, vital motion, sense, reason, soul—thus become one), 5. Soul into knowledge, 6. Knowledge into wisdom, 7. The supernatural passage (*occasus*) of the purified soul (which has now become wisdom) into God (1020). The *five* (which are united in the first four stages) and the *three* (the last three stages) make eight, *supernaturalis cubi perfectissima soliditas*. This mystical eight is prefigured in the title of Psalm vi, *Psalmus David pro octava*[1], and in the Resurrection of our Lord on the eighth day (1021).

---

[1] It may be noted that Chrysostom, *De Compunct.* II. 4, interprets ὑπὲρ τῆς ὀγδόης in the title of Psalm vi, of the Day of Judgment.

This final union with God of the restored creation
through regenerate humanity, this unspeakable consummation of all things in the One, the Perfect, the Eternal, is
the summit of our philosopher's intellectual quest, as it
must be the summit of all human thought and all human
desire. Here he takes his farewell of us with the memorable
words: *"Let every one be fully persuaded in his own mind*,
until the light shall come which makes darkness of the false
light of philosophers, and changes the darkness of those
who think rightly into light."

III. THE PHILOSOPHY OF ERIGENA: AN EXPOSITION

THE most general impression which the system of Erigena leaves upon the mind of the student is that of intellectual vastness. The problem of universal existence is seen in its whole range, reaching from eternity to eternity. The profoundest conceptions of religion and of philosophy are used with an unconstrained freedom, and thought is never checked by anything but the reverence that it owes to itself. Whatever we may think of the permanent value of Erigena's speculations, there can at least be no question as to the vast scale of them, and every one who has read the Scot's great work will agree as to the justice of Vacherot's phrase about "the immense perspectives" of his thought[1].

The first question that presents itself as we study the system of Erigena is concerned with the character of his theistic doctrine. His philosophy is repeatedly characterised as pantheistic, in encyclopaedias, in histories of philosophy, and in histories of dogma. This is often enlarged upon in the obvious direction, and he is made to deny the reality of personality, of freedom, of evil, and even of the world itself. It is easy enough to quote detached passages in apparent

[1] La théologie de Jean Scot, héritière de plus grandes conceptions de l'Église d'Orient, ne convenait pas au Christianisme du moyen âge. Elle ouvrait à la pensée religieuse d'immenses perspectives; elle répandait de hautes clartés sur les problèmes les plus difficiles de la métaphysique chrétienne; elle continuait les traditions de ces magnifiques génies, qui avaient élevé le Christianisme au sommet de la philosophie elle-même. Mais telle lumière était trop éclatante pour les faibles yeux de la scolastique. Vacherot, *Histoire de l'école d'Alexandrie*, III. p. 81.

proof of all this, and indeed it is easy enough to summarise his whole philosophy in a way that seems to justify it. Yet it must be urged that Erigena encounters this criticism, not because he specially deserves it, but because he is the first thinker, and perhaps the only one as yet, to present to the world a complete Christian philosophy. For the system of Erigena, whether adequate or not, is a complete philosophy of existence, and whether orthodox or not, is an essentially Christian one.

Now if there is to be a complete Christian philosophy at all, it must be monistic. Practical religion may be content, for example, with the gaping dualism of good and evil, assuaged by the vague promise of the final victory of good, as in other matters the practical man is content with the naïve realism of matter and mind. But philosophy cannot be content with either. A religious philosophy must look backward to the opening of every breach, and forward to the closing of it. It must give some rationale of the beginning of evil and of the end of it; of the first and final relation to God of all existence; of the creation and consummation of all things. It *must* do this, in regard to the definite teaching of the New Testament, in many passages[1], as well as in deference to the imperious demand of the religious consciousness for unity.

But any such attempt to reduce the universe to one, and to conceive of God as all in all, must at least look pantheistic; it must seem at first sight to abolish evil, to imperil personality, and to volatilise the world. How could it be otherwise? Any scheme of unity, in whatever region of thought or of action, has some appearance of discounting the reality and the importance of existing distinctions; and any thorough-

[1] Rom. xi. 36, 1 Cor. xv. 28, Col. i. 16–17, Eph. iv. 6.

going monism seems, at the first glance, to merge the difference between the Creator and the creation, to minimise the opposition between good and evil, and to blur all the sharp individuality of existing things as they are known to us.

It is therefore natural enough that the doctrine of Erigena should be regarded as pantheistic, upon a superficial acquaintance with it. A closer examination will suggest that if it is pantheism, it is pantheism of an entirely distinct and peculiar type, for while it holds that God is in the world and in all that exists, it also holds that He is above all and beyond all; and if it teaches that God is wholly present in His creation, in its totality and in its parts, it also teaches that nevertheless He abides wholly in Himself[1]. Like most things that are in dispute in the world, it is a matter of definition. If by pantheism we mean (as we ought to do) that the actuality of the universe is taken as one and all, and identified with the Absolute—that the totality of things is taken for God—then Erigena is emphatically not a pantheist[2]. If, on the other hand, any doctrine which holds the essential unity of the Creator and the creation is identified with pantheism, then indeed Erigena is a pantheist, for his doctrine is absolute monism. But it is either confusion of thought or abuse of language to call this pantheism. Almost every form of religion holds some such doctrine, and Christianity distinctly does. In short, if the meaning of the word

[1] Wir hier, wenn mit Pantheismus, doch mit einer ganz eigenthümlichen Form desselben zu thun haben. Es heisst nicht nur, dass Gott in der Welt wird und all ihr Sein ist; es heisst auch, dass er ausser ihr, über ihr, und noch in sich und bei sich ist, und es heisst dann ferner, dass Gott in seiner Schöpfung, in ihrer Totalität sowohl, wie in jedem ihrer Theile, ganz gegenwärtig sei und doch zugleich ganz in sich bleibe. Huber, *Johannes Scotus Erigena*, p. 171.

[2] *Ibid.* pp. 180–1.

be defined with anything like strictness, Erigena is not a pantheist[1].

Considerably less than justice has been done to Erigena in this matter. Some of his critics have taken one half of the Scot's doctrine, and labelled it pantheistic, while leaving out of account the other half, which is as essential to his system of thought, and as emphatic in its manner of expression[2]. It may be urged that the formal reconciliation of the statements on the one side and on the other is difficult, but that is inevitable in any doctrine that deals with infinitude. It is the element of paradox which is inseparable from all mysticism, and all religious philosophy. Any philosophy that attempts to reach the abysmal problems of the infinite and the eternal must tremble on the brink of hopeless contradiction, but as long as the verge is not passed, it has not forfeited its right to be called a philosophy.

It has been the theological tradition of the Christian Church to keep the doctrine of God in equipoise between the opposite poles of the Divine Immanence and the Divine Transcendence. But practically the emphasis has always been more upon the distinctness of God from the world than upon the union of God with the world. Ecclesiastical re-

---

[1] This is the judgment of almost every careful student of Erigena. Thus Erdmann writes: "The accusation of Pantheism which has been made against Erigena's doctrine of evil, is justified only in so far as the latter really avoids dualism more than the opposite extreme." *History of Philosophy*, I. p. 298.

[2] Mr R. L. Poole says, with great justice: "It is impossible for anyone who fairly weighs his opinions on this subject not to feel that the judgment of his pantheism has been premature and warranted only by one set of statements, contradicted and at the same time justified by another set no less necessary to his complete understanding. If the reconciliation appear paradoxical we have but to remember that paradox in the philosopher's view is inevitable when we attempt to conceive the eternal." *Illustrations of the History of Medieval Thought*, pp. 67–68.

ligion has always been in more danger of Deism than of
Pantheism, as, indeed, in respect of all other truth, it has
been in more danger of the mechanical than of the mystical.
It is certain that less than justice has been done to some
great elements of New Testament doctrine, and it is equally
certain that the modern tendency in religious thought is,
and will be, in the direction of redressing the balance[1].

It is the doctrine of Erigena that the essence of God
comes to manifestation in the creation, and yet remains
in God without modification or severance. It appears in
the universe as multiple, visible, and accessible to human
thought, but it is still single, invisible, and incommunicable
in the Divine Nature[2]. So the human spirit manifests itself
in speech and writing, using audible syllables that are
separated in time, and visible letters that are separated in
space, and yet it remains itself undivided, unheard, unseen.
Thus the *processio Dei per omnia* and His *mansio in se ipso*
do not exclude each other. The phrases are the Areopagite's,
borrowed and used by Erigena[3].

The idea of the world as immanent in God is distinguished
from God Himself, on the one hand, and equally dis-

---

[1] "The changes adopted in the methods of theistic proof have all tended in
one direction, namely, to remove or correct extreme and exaggerated conceptions of the divine transcendence, and to produce a true appreciation of the
divine immanence—to set deism aside, and to enrich theism with what is good
in pantheism." Dr Flint, *Agnosticism*, p. 592.

[2] Compare the thought of Dante:

> Vedi l' eccelso omai e la larghezza
>   dell' eterno valor, poscia che tanti
>   speculi fatti s' ha, in che si spezza
> uno manendo in sè, come davanti.
>
>   *Paradiso*, XXIX. 142–5.

[3] *De Div. Nat.* 644 C, and Dionysius, *Ep. ad Titum*, IX. 3.

tinguished from the world of appearance, on the other[1]. Erigena guards himself by these distinctions from that merging of God in the universe, and of the universe in God, which is the essence of pantheism. It may be thought that all these reservations are imperilled[2] by Erigena's doctrine as to the nature of God. For he contends that it is not one thing for God to be, and another thing for Him to think, and another thing for Him to will, but that His nature, His thought, His will, and all else that He is and does, are all one and the same[3]. It has been urged that if the thought of God is not to be distinguished from the nature of God, it becomes impossible to maintain any real distinction between the ideal world, as the thought of God, and God Himself. But Erigena's answer to this, if he were speaking in modern terms, would probably be that the ideal world is said to be the thought of God in the sense that it is the ideal object of the Divine thought, but that it is the act of thought which is not to be distinguished from the act of will in the nature of God, as neither is to be distinguished from that nature itself. It is the thought of God in the sense of *His thinking* that is one with His will and His essence, but

---

[1] *De Div. Nat.* 675 C, 770 C.

[2] Christlieb, *Leben und Lehre des Johannes Scotus Erigena*, pp. 191–2.

[3] This was Augustine's doctrine. "For to Him it is not one thing to *be*, and another thing to live, as though He could *be*, not living; nor is it to Him one thing to live, and another thing to understand, as though He could live, not understanding; nor is it to Him one thing to understand, another thing to be blessed, as though He could understand and not be blessed. But to Him to live, to understand, to be blessed, are to *be*." *De Civ. Dei*, VIII. 6. So also Anselm, *Proslogion*, c. xviii. Compare Thomas Aquinas: *Et sit oportet in Deo esse voluntatem, cum sit in eo intellectus. Et sicut suum intelligere est suum esse, ita et suum esse est suum velle. Summ. Theol.* I. qu. 19, art. I. *Cum Deus sit primum ens, prima causa, actus purus, et ipsum esse, omni prorsus simplicitate gaudet. Summ. Theol.* I. qu. 3, art. 7. See also I. qu. 13, art. 5.

the ideal world is the thought of God in the sense of *the thing which He thinks*.

The whole view of Erigena is in the direction that the existence of the universe is a necessary moment in the life of God, a necessary fulfilment of the process of the Divine Nature, so that if it were possible to conceive of God without the universe eternally grounded in Him, as His eternal thought and His eternal purpose, we should also be left with an impossible conception of the nature of the Deity as unfulfilled and defective. Without the universe, God would be only the *possible* Creator of all, the *potential* Lord of all[1]. In other words, universal existence is not an accidental parergon of the Almighty, the accomplishment of a casual purpose in the mind of God which might conceivably never have existed in His mind, but the necessary fulfilment of what was eternally and essentially in the Divine Nature.

This conception has important consequences in religious thought. Unless the necessity is conceded, the whole of experience becomes infected with a casual and arbitrary character. A universe which might never have existed, and need never have existed, is only an Almighty caprice, after all, and it is not difficult to see that this reduces our moral and spiritual life to a sort of contingency that ultimately robs it of all its passionate and poignant reality. The whole of things can hardly "mean intensely and mean good" unless it is grounded, not in a mere *fiat*, but in the eternal nature

[1] So also Augustine argues. "Wherefore, if God always has been Lord, He has always had creatures under His dominion,—creatures, however, not begotten of Him, but created by Him out of nothing; nor coeternal with Him, for He was before them, though at no time without them, because He preceded them, not by the lapse of time but by His abiding eternity." *De Civ. Dei*, XII. 15. The thought is also found in Origen, *De Princ.* I. 2.

of God[1]. To regard creation otherwise (as a modern philosopher has said) is to "represent the universe as in no way
organic to the divine life[2]."

But the necessity of creation is not a physical or an
external necessity. It is the necessity that belongs to a
moral nature, and therefore it is a free necessity. When
God acts necessarily He still acts freely, for the necessity is
that of His own nature, without any external determination.
The Absolute limits itself, but in accordance with a moral
and rational necessity, for the Absolute is the source of all
that is right and of all that is rational[3]. As the Neoplatonists
used to say, God must necessarily create, as the sun must
shine, and as the flowers must be fragrant. The Eternal
Goodness is creative, and could not be otherwise, in its very
nature.

This doctrine of creation has been criticised generally by
Lotze[4] on the ground that "it leads consistently to nothing
but a thoroughgoing determinism." But he describes it as
the conception which regards the world as "a necessary,
involuntary and inevitable development of the nature of
God." This, surely, is begging the question, at least as far
as our philosopher is concerned. For Erigena held that it
was a necessary development of the nature of God *and
equally of the will of God*: there can be no schism between
what God is and what God wills. And there is no question
of necessity, except the necessity which resides in the
character of God. God, being what He is, must will and

---

[1] Cf. John Caird, *Philosophy of Religion*, pp. 238-9.
[2] A. S. Pringle-Pattison, *The Idea of God in the Light of Recent Philosophy*,
p. 302.
[3] Huber, *Johannes Scotus Erigena*, pp. 254-5.
[4] *Outlines of the Philosophy of Religion*, pp. 71-72.

must create that which is good. But the only constraint is that which makes God true to Himself. The question of human freedom is not involved at all, for that is as conceivable on the supposition that the world exists necessarily as a result of what God eternally is and what God eternally wills, as on the supposition that it exists incidentally as a result of an arbitrary volition of God,—a single act of will unrelated to His essential nature. The last conception, indeed, is surely impossible when once it is plainly represented to the mind. And, apart from early mythology in the book of Genesis, it is more consonant with the teaching of Scripture to think of the work of creation as a continuous and characteristic activity of God[1], than to think of it as a "paroxysm of initiation."

While Erigena insists, with a Platonic emphasis, upon the goodness of God as the essential source of His creative activity, and therefore of the existence of all that is, his doctrine of the superexistence of God leads, on the other hand, to the startling conclusion (which reappears in many of the mystics) that God may be said to be *nothing*—that the Divine Nature, *dum incomprehensibilis intelligitur, per excellentiam nihilum non immerito vocitatur*[2]. The whole of this paradox is precisely equivalent to Mr Bradley's remark that a God who should be capable of existing would be no God at all[3]. Any conception of God which makes Him one of a number of things that exist, a mere item in the catalogue of universal being, is manifestly untenable. The stipulation that He is the greatest of all existences does not save the situation. Our thought of God is wholly inadequate unless it makes Him at once the source and the sum of all that

---

[1] John v. 18.   [2] *De Div. Nat.* 681 A.
[3] *Appearance and Reality*, p. 450.

really is, and therefore greater than all, before all and beyond all. But if He be that we cannot classify Him according to the categories that apply to all else in the universe: the terms of thought that we are compelled to apply to every other existence cannot apply to His existence. This means that His existence is beyond our formal knowledge: we may affirm the existence of God, and we may have a spiritual assurance of it, but we can no more define and express and comprehend His existence than we can the existence of nothingness. The terms *Deus* and *nihil* are therefore logically equal: both express something beyond the pale of existence *as we know it* in the universe. They are equal only in the sense that extremes meet, and Erigena is careful to explain that in another sense there is all the difference in the world between the *nothing* that is so called because it surpasses all knowledge (and therefore *is not* to our finite understanding), and the *nothing* that is mere privation of existence (*nihil de nihilo*). In other words, though the super-existent and the non-existent are worlds apart, yet on the dialectical level they are the same, because neither of them exists as far as our logical understanding is concerned: it is not possible for the mind to formulate the existence of either the one or the other.

Nor is it fair to dismiss language of this kind as empty paradox, or mere subtlety. The persistence of it among the mystics should be enough to warn us of that. As one of the greatest of living philosophers has said, the mystics "did not intend by this rejection of all positive determinations to imply that there was no God, or that God was nothing." It was in the effort to express a boundless positivity that they disallowed all "determinate thoughts of this super-essential, super-rational, super-personal, nay, super-absolute unity that is neither subject nor object and in which all difference begins and ends[1]."

How can that which passes the limits of language, and even of thought, be expressed at all[2]? Manifestly, we can only attempt the expression of it by phrases which are utterly paradoxical, and which, as Fuller said, "do knock at the door of blasphemy, though not always with the intent to enter in thereat." Every possible predicate must be denied of God, as being insufficient to express His unthinkable perfections, and the denial of everything conceivable reduces our thought of God to mere absence of thought, and yet the purpose of the denial is to express more than thought can possibly attain[3]. It is, as Höffding has said, "precisely the inexhaustible positivity which bursts through every conceptual form, and turns every determination into an impossibility[4]."

It has been said that the whole of this trend of thought is merely "a deification of the word 'not[5].'" It is surely more than that, but in any case the criticism will apply

---

[1] James Ward, *Realm of Ends*, p. 35.

[2] *Deus est super omnem essentiam et intelligentiam, cujus neque ratio est, neque intelligentia, neque dicitur, neque intelligitur, neque nomen ejus est, neque verbum. De Div. Nat.* 510 D.

[3] Martensen, while criticising the conception, admits that the Areopagite and Erigena call God *nothing* "not because of His emptiness, but because of His inexpressible fulness, in virtue of which He transcends every *something*." *Christian Dogmatics*, p. 88.

[4] *Philosophy of Religion*, § 21.

[5] It is singular that Professor Watson, while making this criticism, on the next page concedes everything that necessitates and justifies the method of the *theologia negativa*. "As the source and principle of all being, God cannot be identified with any particular form of being. He cannot be simply one being existing side by side with others, but must be conceived as in some sense comprehending within Himself all that is, and therefore *as in His essence higher than the highest of the beings whose existence is dependent upon Him*." *The Philosophical Basis of Religion*, p. 273. The italics are mine.

equally well to every possible statement that can be made about the Absolute, or about God, from the philosophic side. For if we say that God is infinite, we are merely saying that He is not finite; if we say that He is eternal, we are merely saying that He is not temporal. Yet we *mean* more than this. The statements are really negative, and in the very nature of thought and language they cannot be anything else, but the intention of them is positive. They cannot be formally affirmative, for the simple reason that finite minds cannot have formal knowledge of the infinite. If we want to name some particular thing in a foreign language and we do not know the proper name of it in that language, we can only suggest what we mean in one of two ways. So far as our command of the language extends, we can say what the thing is like, or we can say what it is not. So it is in any doctrine of God : we are trying to name the Nameless. We may use the method of metaphor, and say what God is like,—Love, Light, the King of Kings, the Judge of all, the Heavenly Father,—or we may use the method of negation, and say what God is not—not local, not temporal, not limited in knowledge, not limited in power, not existing as any other being exists, not knowing as any other being knows. Now it is obvious that the first method is that of practical religion, and rightly so, for it is the most vivid and the most popular ; but it is equally obvious that metaphor is out of place in meta-physics, and that if we are to make any philosophic statements about God at all, they must be negative in form, that they may suggest a limitless positivity for which we have no other language. We have a positive notion of infinity and of eternity in our minds but we cannot formulate it either in thought or in language, and so we are reduced to negation. It is an example of what Coleridge called "the imbecilities of the understanding" when dealing with the infinite.

The nature of God, in short, is so far beyond the reach of our intellect that it is not possible to say anything of Him that is strictly adequate[1]. Everything that can be said of Him is either metaphorical or negative—either a confessed accommodation to our limited intelligence, or a mere denial of the possibility of adequate knowledge. We cannot know God, therefore, as He is in the eternal mystery of His being: we can only know Him as He is to us; as He has been pleased to make Himself known to us. Erigena's repeated insistence upon this thought sounds very modern[2]. It reminds us again and again of modern tendencies like the Ritschlian theology, and of modern utterances like that of Browning's Pope in *The Ring and the Book*:

> "O Thou, as represented here to me
> In such conception as my soul allows!"

There is here, we think, a profound philosophical justification of orthodox Christianity. We cannot really know anything about God at all beyond a series of vast negations, dimly suggesting a reality which is so measureless that the mind cannot grasp it—unless God has revealed Himself to men in the terms of human personality and life and love. Men cannot worship a formless Infinitude; humanity must have, in the Apostle's language, an Image of the invisible

[1]   E se le fantasie nostre son basse
a tanta altezza, non è maraviglia,
chè sopra il Sol non fu occhio ch' andasse.
Paradiso, x. 46–48.

[2] It is really ancient enough. Cf. Origen, *De Princ.* I.; Basil, *Adv. Eun.* I. 12; John Damascene, *De Fide Orth.* I. 2. 4; Augustine, *De Doct. Christ.* I. 6, and many other places.

God. There can be no real, living, satisfying knowledge of God unless it is a knowledge of God manifest in the flesh. It is a great phrase which Irenaeus quotes from some unknown writer: "He spoke well who said that the immeasurable (*immensum*) Father is measured (*mensuratum*) in the Son[1]."

Erigena's doctrine of the *se ipsum ignorare* of God means, as he himself epigrammatically expresses it, that "God does not know *what* He is because He is not a 'what.'" *Deus itaque nescit se, quid est, quia non est quid*[2]. That is, the Divine Nature, being beyond all resemblances and differences, cannot be known, either by itself or by another, in any categorical form. The whole process of human knowledge consists in the translation of the perceptual into the conceptual; in the reference of a known fact to its place in the system of known facts; in the classifying of a "that" as a "what." But this process of knowledge is plainly impossible in regard to God; He cannot be allocated a place in a universal system of existence every part of which conditions every other, for the very character of His existence must be that it is unconditioned, that He is before and beyond every system of existence, as well as the source and principle of all existence. All formal knowledge is thus a process of cataloguing and classifying, and God cannot be catalogued and classified. He knows Himself, but He cannot either know Himself or be known in the usual terms

---

[1] *Contra Haer.* IV. 4. 2.

[2] *Deus itaque nescit se, quid est, quia non est quid: incomprehensibilis quippe in aliquo et sibi ipsi et omni intellectui....Nescit igitur, quid ipse est, hoc est, nescit se quid esse, quoniam cognoscit, se nullum eorum, quae in aliquo cognoscuntur, et de quibus potest dici vel intelligi, quid sunt, omnino esse. De Div. Nat.* 589 B, C.

of relational knowledge. He cannot know *quid est* for the sufficient reason, *non est quid.*

This doctrine of the Divine Ignorance, therefore, like that of the Divine Nothingness, is an attempt to express the inexpressible—an attempt to set forth the fact that God must know in a way that is beyond all conceivable knowledge, as He must exist in a way that is beyond all conceivable existence. Logically, ignorance is the equation of inconceivable knowledge, as nothingness is the equation of inconceivable existence. However paradoxical Erigena's expression of these truths may be, there can be no doubt that they are implicit in every system of theology, and that they must be emphasised in every system of religious philosophy.

The chill sterility which besets the Neoplatonist conception of God as the Superessential Unity is largely escaped, in Erigena's system, by his treatment of the doctrine of the Trinity.

He conceives of the Trinity as the life-process of the Deity, the self-birth of God. It is not a process that begins and ends, but an ever-present and eternal act[1]. The Son is eternally begotten of the Father and the Spirit eternally proceeds from the Father, through the Son. The existence of God is therefore represented as a *life*—not as the bare unity of abstract being, but (in the Scot's own phrase) as "a fruitful multiplicity[2]."

The doctrine of the Trinity found in both Dionysius and Erigena has been criticised as making the distinctions in the Godhead merely subjective. It is argued that Erigena's contention as to the inapplicability of the Aristotelian

[1] Huber, *Johannes Scotus Erigena*, p. 198.
[2] *De Div. Nat.* 456 B.

categories to the Divine Nature (especially the category of relation and the connected one of habitude) results in the conclusion that there is no hypostatic distinction in the Godhead, but only a difference of mere name[1]. This seems particularly shallow. Neither the Areopagite nor the Scot would have dreamt of denying that these distinctions represented eternal realities, but they would have denied (and so, surely, would every competent theologian of every age and school) that any human definition can be an adequate expression of those eternal realities.

With the whole Church Dionysius and Erigena confessed the Deity to be a Trinity in Unity, but they went on to affirm that God is more than Unity and more than Trinity (*plusquam unitas est, et plusquam trinitas*)[2]. Precisely in the same way they taught that God is ὑπεράγαθος, ὑπεραγαθότης. It would be as fair to argue from those terms that Erigena denied the goodness of God as to argue that he denied the Trinity. But when he taught that God is more-than-good and more-than-goodness it is precisely the point in the paradox of Angelus Silesius: "Gott ist nicht tugendhaft: aus Ihm kommt Tugend her, Wie aus der Sonn' die Strahlen, und Wasser aus dem Meer[3]." God is not good merely in the sense of the ordinary antithesis between good and evil, but, as the source and sum of goodness, He is more than good. So, God is not One and Three merely in the ordinary

[1] Es findet also zwischen den Personen der Trinität keine wirkliche Beziehung, kein reales Verhältniss statt. Warum? Weil unter den Personen der Trinität keine reale, substanzielle Wesen, keine hypostatischen Unterschiede, sondern blosse Namen und Verhältnisse zu verstehen sind. Christlieb, *Leben und Lehre des Johannes Scotus Erigena*, p. 182. A similar criticism appears in more than one English writer, e.g. W. R. Inge, *The Philosophy of Plotinus*, II. p. 112, and R. L. Ottley, *The Doctrine of the Incarnation*, II. p. 168.
[2] *De Div. Nat.* 614 C.
[3] *Der cherubinische Wandersmann*, v. 50.

arithmetical sense, in which one is a third of three, and three is the sum of three units, but His Unity is more than Unity, and His Trinity is more than Trinity. Erigena never really questions (at least in these regions) what is positive in orthodox doctrine ; he is only concerned to deny that any human language can be adequate to define God, or any human thought to comprehend Him. The Areopagite is merely emphasising the same truth when he says epigrammatically : "All human thought is a kind of error, when tried by the stability and durability of the Divine and most perfect conceptions[1]." Augustine is expressing it again when he says that "God is more truly thought than He is uttered, and He exists more truly than He is thought[2]."

The supreme revelation of God to mankind is in Christ. The doctrine of the Incarnation is conceived along the line of Greek patristic thought, and in the light of Pauline passages like 1 Cor. xv. 28, Eph. i. 10, and Col. i. 20. It is a reconciliation and a reunion of the whole creation with God. There are two poles of unity, so to speak—the creation is one in God at the first, through the original union of the primal causes in the Logos, and it will be one again at the last through the reunion of all things in humanity as redeemed in Christ. The Incarnation is therefore, metaphysically, the realisation of the uniting principle in Christ, the ideal man, and then, by consequence, in ideal humanity, as redeemed in Christ. Evil is the principle of division, and Christ is the principle of reunion.

It has been said that Erigena regards Christ as the

---

[1] πᾶσα ἀνθρωπίνη διάνοια πλάνη τίς ἐστι, κρινομένη πρὸς τὰ σταθερὸν καὶ μόνιμον τῶν θείων καὶ τελειοτάτων νοήσεων. De Div. Nom. VII. 1. (865 B, Vol. 3, ed. Migne.)

[2] Verius enim cogitatur Deus quam dicitur, et verius est quam cogitatur. De Trin. VII. 4.

Redeemer "less through what He did, than through what He was: all the other acts of His earthly life, in their significance for the redemption of the world, depend upon the one fact of the Incarnation[1]." This is true enough, but it is merely saying in other words what is written large over all Erigena's writings, that he is following the Christological tradition of the East, rather than of the West. Latin theology tended to make the Incarnation merely a necessary prelude to the Atonement, and the redeeming act was conceived as practically limited to the Cross. God became man that He might die for man, and it was by His death that man is saved from sin. Greek theology, on the other hand, regarded the Incarnation "as the completion and the crown of a spiritual process in the history of man, dating from the creation[2]," of which Christ's redeeming death was indeed the climax, but the Cross did not represent the whole process, and it did not comprise the whole fact of redemption. The birth of Christ, His life, His spirit, His obedience, were all part of the redeeming act. To the theologians of the Eastern Church the very fact that God became man, apart from the actual content of His earthly life, was itself a redemptive event, with consequences for the whole creation. The whole of the Logos doctrine, in fact, counted for much more in the East than in the West.

Moreover, it is not only true that here, as everywhere, Erigena is under the influence of the theology of the East, but this is a point at which he is particularly indebted to what may be called the main tradition of Greek orthodoxy.

[1] Kurz Erlöser ist Christus weniger durch sein Thun, als durch sein Sein: gegenüber der einen That seines Menschgewordenseins treten alle andern Thatsachen seines irdischen Lebens in ihrer Bedeutung für die Erlösung zurück. Christlieb, *Leben und Lehre des Johannes Scotus Erigena*, p. 396.

[2] A. V. G. Allen, *The Continuity of Christian Thought*, p. 176.

For it is precisely here that the influence of Maximus and Gregory Nazianzen has overpowered the influence of the Areopagite. There can be no doubt that Christ is much more central in the system of Erigena than in that of the pseudo-Dionysius. The fact of the Incarnation is, indeed, so essential to Erigena's thought that it gives a different significance to both God and man from that which is found in the purer Neoplatonism of the Areopagite. God cannot realise His Nature in its perfection apart from man; nor man his, apart from God. The Creation is a necessary fulfilment of the Divine Nature, and all is created in man. Man is the image of God and is only himself when he is in essential union with God.

This is a very distinct and momentous modification of the doctrine of the Neoplatonists, and it is essentially a Christian modification. It is mainly due to Maximus[1]. From him Erigena's thought in this direction derived both a more Christian and a more ethical character, as contrasted with that of the Areopagite.

The system of Erigena is essentially Christo-centric, for the universe is conceived as created in Christ and restored in Christ. But it is the metaphysical Logos rather than the historic Jesus who is mostly in Erigena's thoughts. Therefore Dorner has some justification in declaring that for our philosopher Christ is merely "an ideal Figure, a universal relation between cause and actuality, and has no significance

---

[1] In der eigenthümlichen Stellung und Bedeutung, welche Erigena dem Menschen in seinem System gibt, reisst er sich von dem immer noch überwiegenden Platonismus los, um zu dem entgegensetzen Standpunct überzugehen. Baur, *Lehre v. d. Dreieinigkeit*, II. p. 295. Dies ist der Hauptpunct, in welchem Maximus der vermittelnde Uebergang von dem Areopagiten zu Erigena ist. *Ibid.* p. 268.

for a real redemption[1]." But it ought to be remembered
that Christianity has a metaphysical aspect, and that it is
only natural that the philosophic side of religion should be
uppermost in a philosophy.

It is not to be denied that there is an absence of all
historic sense in Erigena's references to Christ. The events
related in the Gospels are accepted, and mystical expositions are based upon them, but there is never any real
appreciation of the human and historic element in Christianity. This is what we should expect, and Erigena can
scarcely be blamed for it. It was a disability that he shared
with every mediaeval writer, and, indeed, we might go much
further than that. But it was qualified by one marked
characteristic—a personal devotion to our Lord that is
plainly both fervent and sincere. We find touching evidence
of this in a few prayers and ejaculations that are interspersed,
like living springs, amid the arid wastes of metaphysical
dialogue. "O God, our salvation and redemption, Who hast
given us our nature, freely bestow upon us also Thy grace;
show Thy light amid the shadows of ignorance to those
who seek Thee and pant after Thee; recall us from our
errors; reach forth Thy right arm to the weak, unable
without Thee to come to Thee; reveal Thyself to those who
desire nothing except Thyself[2]." "Take Christ from me, and
no good will remain to me, no torment will terrify me. To
be deprived of Christ, and absent from Him—this, and none
other, is the real torment of every rational creature[3]."
"O Lord Jesus, none other prize, none other blessedness,
none other joy, do I ask of Thee, but that I may rightly and

---

[1] Dorner, *Lehre von der Person Christi*, II. p. 354.

[2] *De Div. Nat.* 650 B.

[3] *Ibid.* 989 A.

purely understand Thy words, which are inspired by Thy Spirit[1]!"

It is noteworthy that in his eschatological doctrine Erigena makes an emphatic distinction between the union of the manhood of Christ with God, and the unification of the rest of humanity with God, through Christ. He is careful to maintain the difference in phrase as well as in principle, and uses *deificari* of men and *in Deitatem mutari* of the humanity of Christ[2].

On the doctrine of the Procession of the Holy Spirit, Erigena adopts a mediating theory. It was the one doctrinal question at issue between the Eastern and the Western Church, and it happened that Erigena, the most learned man and the most subtle thinker alive in the West, was essentially Greek in all his theological sympathies. He held that the Spirit proceeded from (*ex*) the Father through (*per*) the Son, as the Love uniting both, and as the Gift given by both. *Est enim Spiritus amborum, quoniam ex Patre per Filium procedit, et est donum utriusque, quoniam ex Patre per Filium donatur, et est amor utriusque, Patrem et Filium jungens*[3]. This is precisely the doctrine of John of Damascus, who used the metaphor of the sun, the ray, and the light[4], beloved by Erigena, and held that the Spirit was the Spirit of the Son, not as proceeding from the Son (ἐκ τοῦ Υἱοῦ) but as proceeding from the Father (ἐκ τοῦ Πατρός) through the Son (δι' Υἱοῦ)[5].

This was also the doctrine of the formula of union at the

---

[1] *De Div. Nat.* 1010 B.   [2] *Ibid.* 911 B.   [3] *Ibid.* 603 A.

[4] He got it from Gregory Nazianzen. πάλιν ἥλιον ἐνεθυμήθην, καὶ ἀκτῖνα, καὶ φῶς. *Orat.* XXXI. It is found also in Tertullian, *Adv. Prax.* 8.

[5] *De Fide Orthodoxa,* I. 8. But the formula *a Patre per Filium* is found in some of the Latin Fathers long before the age of the Damascene. See Tertullian, *Adv. Prax.* 4, and Augustine, *De Trin.* XV. 48.

Council of Florence in 1439, which established a brief peace between the Eastern and the Western Churches. The *filioque* was retained, and the Procession was defined as *ex Patre per Filium*[1].

This conception of the Trinity becomes the fundamental principle of creation. The Father, in His eternal self-subsistence, is the ultimate source of all existence; the Son, as the Wisdom and the Word of God, is the source of all creative power and possibility; the Spirit, as proceeding from the Father through the Son, is the source of all the diverse actuality of the created universe[2]. What the Father wills, the Son creates, and the Spirit perfects[3]. All that exists bears the mark of this triune origin. The *essentia* ($o\dot{v}\sigma\acute{\iota}a$) of the Father, the *virtus* ($\delta\acute{v}\nu\alpha\mu\iota\varsigma$) of the Son, and the *operatio* ($\dot{\epsilon}\nu\acute{\epsilon}\rho\gamma\epsilon\iota a$) of the Spirit are present throughout the whole creation. But it is in the nature of man, as made in the image of God, that this is most clearly discerned. The *essentia, virtus, operatio* appear in man as *intellectus, ratio, sensus interior* ($\nu o\hat{v}\varsigma$, $\lambda\acute{o}\gamma o\varsigma$, $\delta\iota\acute{a}\nu o\iota a$). These again are made to correspond with Augustine's triad, *esse, velle, scire*, since the *virtus* of the rational nature is to *will* what is right, and the *operatio* of the rational nature is to *know* itself and God, as far as these can be known.

While this doctrine of the Trinity as the creative *schema* of the universe is steadily maintained, the greatest emphasis

---

[1] Hagenbach, *History of Doctrines*, I. p. 502. Popoff, *History of the Council of Florence*, p. 130.

[2] The relation is well summarised by Christlieb, *Leben und Lehre des Johannes Scotus Erigena*, p. 242 : " Der Vater ist das Princip der Substanz der)inge, der Sohn das ihrer idealen Ursachen, der Geist das ihrer realen, oesonderen, räumlichen und zeitlichen Erscheinung."

[3] Gregory Nazianzen has a very similar expression : $\kappa a\grave{\iota}\ \tau\grave{o}\ \dot{\epsilon}\nu\nu\acute{o}\eta\mu a\ \ddot{\epsilon}\rho\gamma o\nu\ \mathring{\eta}\nu$, $\lambda\acute{o}\gamma\omega\ \sigma\upsilon\mu\pi\lambda\eta\rho o\acute{v}\mu\epsilon\nu o\nu\ \kappa a\grave{\iota}\ \pi\nu\epsilon\acute{v}\mu a\tau\iota\ \tau\epsilon\lambda\epsilon\iota o\acute{v}\mu\epsilon\nu o\nu$. *Orat.* XXXVIII. 9.

is placed upon that part of it which regards the Logos as the unity and the aggregate of the *causae primordiales*. This doctrine of the primal causes is one of the most characteristic features of Erigena's philosophy. The source of it is undoubtedly the Platonic doctrine of ideas, as developed in the Neoplatonists, and passing thence into the writings of Dionysius. A passage in *The Divine Names* (v. 8) is unquestionably the formal source of Erigena's doctrine. There is an instructive parallel between Erigena's teaching as to the relation of the Logos to the *causae primordiales*, and the doctrine of the Neoplatonists as to the relation of the νοῦς and the κόσμος νοητός, for in both cases the one is regarded as the unity and the aggregate of the other—in both cases, that is to say, there is an attempt to reconcile, by the device of intermediate principles, the unity of the spiritual source and the multiplicity of the phenomenal world, since the intermediate world of spiritual causes is regarded as one, on the higher side, and multiplex, on the lower side. But it must be remembered that Neoplatonist doctrine was unknown to Erigena in its own phrases : he knew it only as it passed into the writings of Origen, Augustine, the pseudo-Dionysius and Maximus.

There is no doubt that one of the most serious philosophical difficulties in Erigena's system is precisely that "ugly broad ditch" with which Schelling taunted Hegel. It is the passage from the One to the Many, from the abstract unity of the world-principle in the Logos to the manifoldness of actual existence. It is significant that this is the cardinal difficulty in each of the most complete systems of idealism that the world has known. The "ideas" of Plato are conceived sometimes as abstract generalisations, and sometimes as creative principles, and it is only the alternation from one sense to the other that enables the philosopher to bridge the gulf between the ideal and the real[1]. In a precisely similar way, Erigena's primordial causes are sometimes used as if they were purely intellectual abstractions and sometimes as if they were active forces which really constitute the world as we know it. The case of Hegel is similar, and it has been said that with him we need "to be on our guard against the idea that logical abstractions can *thicken*, as it were, into real existence[2]."

Erigena would seem to have been instinctively aware of this weakness in his system, if we may judge by the involved and ingenious scheme of relations that he introduces between the primal causes and the real world. Dr Martineau once warned us against allowing scientists to "crib causation by inches," and the warning was wise, for if we substitute for a direct act of creation a long period of evolution it does not in the least relieve us of the task of finding a beginning and a cause; though if you make the period long enough, and the causal sequences which intervene numerous enough, it almost looks as if it did. Now

---

[1] "We cannot doubt that Plato meant to set forth in Ideas not merely the archetypes and essences of all true existence, but energetic powers; that he regarded them as living and active, intelligent and reasonable." Zeller, *Plato and the Older Academy*, p. 267. So also Jowett, *The Dialogues of Plato*, II. p. 13.

[2] "We require to be on our guard against the idea that logical abstractions can *thicken*, as it were, into real existences. Categories are not the skeleton round which an indefinite 'materiature' gathers to form a thing. The meanest thing that exists has a life of its own, absolutely unique and individual, which we can partly *understand* by terms borrowed from our own experience, but which is no more identical with, or in any way like, the description we give of it, than our own inner life is identical with the description we give of it in a book of philosophy. Existence is one thing, knowledge is another." A.S. Pringle-Pattison, *Hegelianism and Personality*, pp. 125–6. But it is fairly obvious that unless our inner life, or anything else, is in some way like the description we give of it, our description is not a description at all.

Erigena appears to have been cribbing actuality by inches. There is the Divine Nature, one, eternal, immutable, and utterly beyond speech or thought. Then there is the Logos, one with God, and yet the unity and the aggregate of the primordial causes. Then there are these causes, as separately conceived. Then there are the substances, which are not very adequately defined. Then, from the blending of these with quantity and quality and so forth, there arise the general elements of the world (which are still immaterial). Then from the interaction of the qualities of these there come the real elements which again blend into the existing world[1]. It is evident that Erigena had an instinctive feeling that the multiplication of intermediate principles and inter-acting agencies made it easier to conceive the passage from the abstract eternal unity of God to the actual temporal multiplicity of the world.

This is, of course, a characteristic feature of Neoplatonism. That type of thought always puts an infinite distance between God and the world, and then seeks to bridge the distance by a series of mediating terms[2]. The tendency is distinctly foreshadowed in the *Timaeus*[3].

It has been said, by an eminent historian of philosophy, that "the fundamental idea, and at the same time the funda-mental error, in Erigena's doctrine is the idea that the

---

[1] This last is a singular approach to one line of modern speculation, which has much to recommend it in recent discoveries in physics—the thought (as Dr Mackenzie expresses it) "that everything is essentially Form, and that the particular—the Matter or the 'that'—is simply a point at which certain universals or orders meet or intersect one another. If this is granted, we have got a considerable way towards the determination of the essential nature of the world as known." *Elements of Constructive Philosophy*, p. 137.

[2] E. Caird, *Evolution of Theology in the Greek Philosophers*, II. p. 266.

[3] J. Adam, *The Religious Teachers of Greece*, p. 372.

degrees of abstraction correspond with the degrees of real existence. He hypostatises the *Tabula Logica*[1]." But a phrase like this hardly disposes of the matter. Where do we get our logical abstractions? They are abstracted from actual existence, and not only so, but they are abstracted precisely because they seem to be the most general and the most essential characteristics of actual existence. The actuality of the universe does, as a matter of fact, embody these attributes. The degrees of abstraction do correspond, in some sense, with the degrees of real existence. They are already somehow hypostatised in the world—unless we are prepared to accept the standpoint of an extreme nominalism (and ultimately of an absolute scepticism) and believe that they are a fiction of the human mind, without any relation to objective reality. But if we believe that we have got them out of actual existence that obviously means that in some way they were already there. What does this mean, again, but that our logical abstractions (in so far as they are properly abstracted from real existence) are in some sense the immaterial scaffolding of the universe, and that things do materialise around this intelligible framework? So Erigena thought[2], and there are recent discoveries and speculations that might be held to point in this direction.

This is, and must be, the point where every system of idealism is logically weakest. But it is also the point where a Christian philosophy will suffer least from its lack of logical demonstration. For one large assumption underlies the philosophy of Erigena, and every system of idealism, and it is an assumption that is only defensible, in the last resort, as an act of faith. The idealist assumes the rationality

---

[1] Ueberweg, *History oj Philosophy*, I. p. 360.
[2] Prantl, *Geschichte der Logik in Abendlande*, II. p. 30.

of the universe. He assumes that there is a real correspond-
ence between being and knowledge; that the universe
discovered by thought is a universe designed by thought;
in short, that the rational is the real, and the real the
rational. That assumption is really implied in the very
possibility of knowledge. We cannot think at all without
assuming that our thoughts are to be trusted to bring us
into contact with reality, and that the universe is such that
we shall not be "put to permanent intellectual confusion[1]."
Now this is purely an act of faith in the reasonableness of
the universe, and that is only another way of saying that it
is an act of faith in God. It is true that this is often enough
unrealised, and that our implicit faith in the reliability of
our own minds, and in the intelligibility of the universe,
does not always, or often, lead on to an explicit faith in
God. Logically, it ought to do so—at least to an explicit
faith in God as *mens mundi*, whether we get any further or
not. But when that express faith in God exists, as a
religious fact, it must strengthen the whole structure of an
idealist philosophy[2]. For if we believe to begin with that
the world represents the thought of God, and that man
was made in the image of God, thinking His thoughts after
Him, it becomes a religious postulate rather than a philosophical assumption which makes us believe not merely
that thought reflects reality, but that it underlies reality,
and that so long as thought is true to itself it must be true
to reality.

This does not justify all the details of Erigena's speculative cosmology, but, from his own point of view, it does
warrant his method in general. That is to say, it warrants

---

[1] Stewart and Tait, *The Unseen Universe*, p. 88.
[2] Cf. Martensen, *Christian Dogmatics*, p. 3.

the Christian idealist in arguing from thought to reality as well as from reality to thought. If our logical abstractions have been properly thinned down, so to speak, from real existence in the first place, it is justifiable to suppose that, in the reverse direction, and on the infinite scale, they *can* "thicken, as it were, into real existence," to use the phrase that has been already quoted. In other words—allowing for the fallibility of human thought in particulars, but assuming a real kinship between the mind of God and the mind of man—if an intellectual analysis of the universe is possible to the mind of man, it must be as the reverse of a process in the mind of God which is not utterly dissimilar, however much larger the scale, and however much more profound the activity. And such a process is the eternal act of creation, according to the doctrine of Erigena[1].

Next to the primal causes, in the descending scale of existence, are the substances. These are regarded as the grounds of individual existence, within the primal causes, which are the most universal grounds of being. The substance is divided (but only in our thought) into genera, species, and individuals. As every individual is contained within its species, so every species is contained within its genus, and every genus within its substance, which exists unchangeably and eternally in the primal causes. As the

[1] After writing this, I encountered Dr Ward's suggestion that if we imagine ourselves actively positing objects in an intellective way, instead of passively perceiving objects in a sensory way, and further imagine, on the level of the understanding, an original thesis instead of a discursive synthesis, we should have a power of "intellective intuition" which would be creation. (*The Realm of Ends*, p. 234.) This, applied to the mind of God, is practically Erigena's conception of creation.

It is closely parallel to Kant's notion of "intellectual intuition," which would create both the form and the matter—a mind of which the ideas would also be the objects. (*Critique of Pure Reason*, p. 43.)

primal causes subsist within the Word of God, so the substances subsist within the primal causes.

The substances are thus at once in God, and in the world of created things. But while the substance is one, it is seen by the human intellect as two, for we are compelled to think of it in one sense as existing in God, simplex, unchangeable, beyond all understanding; and in another sense as existing in the actual world, where quantity, quality, and so forth gather around it, and render it, in a way, accessible to our understanding and our senses. But whether under one aspect or the other, it still remains essentially inconceivable.

Erigena distinguishes between primary accidents and "accidents of accidents." Primary accidents derive from the primary substance, but secondary accidents derive from local and temporal combinations of the primary *essentia*, as, for example, colour. Hence Erigena's conception of substance is variable. Everything is accident in relation to the primary substance, but the primary accidents are themselves substances in relation to the "accidents of accidents." This is like Aristotle's variable use of matter and form, according to which wood, for example, is form in the growing tree, and matter in the house being built[1].

Erigena borrowed his doctrine of matter from Gregory of Nyssa[2]. Matter, lacking form and colour, is bodiless (...*cum*

---

[1] Christlieb, *Leben und Lehre des Johannes Scotus Erigena*, p. 256.

[2] The most relevant passages in the *De Hominis Opificio* of Gregory of Nyssa (which Erigena always calls *De Imagine*) are the following : πᾶσαν γὰρ εὑρήσωμεν ἐκ ποιοτήτων τινῶν συνεστῶσαν τὴν ὕλην, ὧν εἰ γυμνωθείη καθ᾽ ἑαυτήν, οὐδαμοῦ τῷ λόγῳ καταληφθήσεται. (212 D, Vol. 44, ed. Migne.)

ὡς γὰρ οὐκ ἔστι σῶμα, ᾧ τὸ χρῶμα, καὶ τὸ σχῆμα, καὶ ἡ ἀντιτυπία καὶ ἡ διάστασις, καὶ τὸ βάρος, καὶ τὰ λοιπὰ τῶν ἰδιωμάτων οὐ πρόσεστιν, ἕκαστον δὲ τούτων σῶμα οὐκ ἔστιν, ἀλλ᾽ ἕτερόν τι παρὰ τὸ σῶμα, κατὰ τὸ ἰδιάζον εὑρίσκεται· οὕτω κατὰ τὸ ἀντίστροφον, ὅπου δ᾽ ἂν συνδράμῃ τὰ εἰρημένα, τὴν σωματικὴν ὑπόστασιν ἀπεργάζεται. (213 B, Vol. 44, ed Migne.)

ipsa materia, carens forma atque colore, omnino invisibilis sit et incorporea)[1]. It is a kind of medium between existence and non-existence, a movement of non-being seeking to become being[2]. *Nil enim est aliud rerum informitas nisi motus quidam, non esse omnino deserens, et statum suum in eo, quod vere est, appetens*[3]. This formless matter is a very attenuated notion: in the language of Augustine, from whom Erigena borrowed the doctrine, it is *prope nihil*, next to nothing. It is little more than mere formlessness, conceived as the possibility of form.

What then is form? Erigena distinguishes substantial form, which is the idea of any particular being as existing in the mind of God, and qualitative form, which is the characteristic figure of any particular being, arising from the union of quality and quantity: this last is bound up with matter, and is liable to development and destruction, and where it is lacking there is deformity. The substantial form of man, for example, is the idea of man in the mind of God. The qualitative form of man is the characteristic shape and upright position of the human body, as distinguished from the different shape and bent posture of the animals. It is the qualitative form that actualises the corporeal. Οὐσία, quantity and quality are present in every natural body, but they are invisible, until quantity and quality manifest themselves in a visible *quantum* and *quale*. The qualitative form is dependent upon the substantial form, and is a further particularisation of it. The corporeal is a collocation of accidents of οὐσία, and if these are taken away, it ceases to exist. Though it is the combination of

[1] *De Div. Nat.* 662 D.
[2] Huber, *Johannes Scotus Erigena*, pp. 268–270.
[3] *De Div. Nat.* 547 B.

the incorporeal which constitutes the corporeal, the former does not cease to be in the process, and does not even cease to possess its immutable rest; as shadows are made out of light and bodies, but the light and the bodies do not give up their own existence to make the shadows, and when the shadows disappear we know that they are resolved once more into light and bodies, neither of which have been modified in any way by the existence of the shadows. As Huber remarks, the idealism of Erigena appears in the boldest way in this fine metaphor[1].

When Erigena's doctrine of matter was so boldly idealistic why did he burden himself with the notion of formless matter? There was no logical need for it, when materiality was held to arise out of the concourse of immaterial qualities. By his own beautiful metaphor of the shadow, which is caused by the mutual presence of the light and of a body, and yet is neither light nor body, and which, when it disappears, is resolved into its causes, we are led to expect that he will teach that matter, when the concourse of immaterial qualities is dissolved, simply disappears, being resolved into its causes, like the shadow, and leaving nothing behind. Indeed, he does teach this in effect. And yet he clings to the notion of formless matter, which cannot be known either by sense or intellect, and which is, in Augustine's phrase, *prope nihil*, next to nothing.

There is no doubt that Erigena's doctrine of formless matter is due to his respect for patristic and philosophic authority. He found it in Augustine and in Dionysius. The notion seems to be the relic of earlier Greek philosophy, with its universal assumption of a chaos of crude matter,

[1] In dem zuletzt angeführten Beispiel bricht der Idealismus des Erigena am allerkühnsten durch. Huber, *Johannes Scotus Erigena*, p. 285.

which later became a cosmos of ordered matter, so to speak. The later idealism had refined this *materia prima* down to mere formlessness, but had not dispensed with it altogether. Augustine, though he held the doctrine of creation out of nothing (as Erigena did), still held to the notion of formless matter, which he had learned from the Neoplatonists. From Augustine and Dionysius (whose doctrine had the same sources), it passed into Erigena's philosophy, where it is a mere excrescence.

Sometimes he makes it mean nothing more than the mere possibility of form, equivalent to the mere potentiality of matter. So expressed, it cannot be challenged from his point of view. That would be precisely Aristotle's doctrine. But it should be remembered that Erigena and the earlier mediaeval writers knew Aristotle only as a logician[1], and that the doctrine of formless matter came to them not directly from Aristotle but through the medium of Augustine. In the process it had suffered a change. This earlier tradition in mediaeval philosophy was displaced by Thomas Aquinas, who came under the full influence of Aristotle, and who consistently treats the *materia prima* as pure potentiality[2]. But the Augustinian tradition taught that the *materia prima* was not pure potentiality, but possessed some sort of positive actuality, independent of any substantial form[3]. There are many passages in Erigena in which he speaks in this tone.

---

[1] M. de Wulf, *Histoire de la philosophie médiévale*, p. 156. E. Gilson, *Le Thomisme*, p. 17.

[2] *Summa Theol.* Pt. I. qu. 4, art. 1; Pt. I. qu. 7, art. 2, ad. 3; Pt. I. qu. 54, art. 3. *Comm. in librum octavum Metaphysicorum*, XX. 514 A, etc.

[3] L'augustinisme enseigne que la matière première n'est pas une pure potentialité, mais une actualité positive, quoique infime. Mandonnet, *Siger de Brabant et l'Averroïsme latin au XIIIme Siècle*, p. 57. See also de Wulf, *Le Traité de Unitate Formae de Gilles de Lessines*, p. 15.

Now if the *materia prima* be actualised or hypostatised in any degree Erigena's idealistic doctrine of matter is at once in peril, for it is then not alone the concourse of immaterial qualities that constitutes matter, but there is another factor, and a more primary one—formless matter conceived not as a mere potentiality, but as an actual *somewhat*, however attenuated.

There is nothing specially original in Erigena's doctrine of Time and Space. Time begins to be with the world. *Tempus siquidem inter cetera, quae facta sunt, factum est, non autem procreatum, sed concreatum*[1]. It is the measure of the movement of things from their issue out of nothingness, until they reach a state of rest, which will be changeless. Without movement, time would not exist, and without body, space would not exist. Space, like time, is coexistent with the world: it did not exist before the world was created, and it will not exist when the world has ended. Space is immaterial: it is defined as that in which the size of bodies is extended[2]. Space and time are inseparable.

On these points Erigena's doctrine has been sometimes described as an anticipation of Kant[3]. That is going much too far. There is no passage in Erigena's writings that develops any doctrine of time and space beyond the point where Augustine left it, or that anticipates Kant's special doctrine of time and space as forms of perception. To Erigena time and space inhere in the material universe, rather than in the human mind, though they are *in animo*

---

[1] *Homil.* 287 C. This is precisely Augustine's doctrine. *Mundus non in tempore sed cum tempore factus est. De Civ. Dei*, XI. 6. The thought is really Plato's; it occurs in the *Timaeus* (38).

[2] *De Div. Nat.* 889 D.

[3] Christlieb, *Leben und Lehre des Johannes Scotus Erigena*, p. 457.

in the sense that they are our mental measurement of material motion and material extension. He says, again and again, borrowing Augustine's language, that time and space are created with the world and cease with the world. He does not say that they coexist with the mind of man, but with the world of appearance. In short, there is nothing to show that Erigena held the ideality of time and space in the Kantian sense, the peculiarity of which is to "resolve the coexistence and succession of objects into the constitution of the subject[1]."

The most curious detail about Erigena's doctrine of space is that he constantly connects place (*locus*) and definition (*definitio*). He cannot disconnect the spatial sense and the mental sense of *definitio*. There is, of course, a real parallel between the different senses of the word, which etymologically accounts for their existence. To define anything intellectually is to set limits to its meaning, to mark it off from other things, and so to establish its *place* in the world of knowledge. But to the modern mind it seems odd that Erigena should have been unable to separate the original sense of physical delimitation from the metaphorical sense of exact signification. He consistently connects the one with the other[2], and even in his eschatology, when he is declaring that space will cease with the world, he expressly exempts space in the sense of intellectual definition. *Locus et tempus peribunt. Locum nunc dico non rerum definitionem, quae semper manet in animo, sed spatium, quo corporum quantitas extenditur*[3].

---

[1] Martineau, *A Study in Spinoza*, p. 144.
[2] Auf diesen Zusammenhang zwischen Definition und räumlicher Beschränkung kommt er oft zurück. Ritter, *Geschichte der Philosophie*, III. p. 226.
[3] *De Div. Nat.* 889 D.

It is manifest that the philosophy of Erigena, like that of Spinoza, carries some of its last results hidden in its first axioms. Erigena's whole scheme of thought, and particularly his distinction between God and the universe, and his doctrine of evil, depends upon his definition of Nature, as including both *ea quae sunt, et ea quae non sunt,* and upon his further definition of the five modes of Non-being[1]. The most universal conception of Being is a conception so bare of all differentiation that it is upon the same logical level as that of Non-being. Here we have the point of departure of the Hegelian logic[2], according to which pure abstraction, i.e. pure indefinite Being, which lies at the beginning of all, in its absolute indefiniteness and utter lack of content, is indistinguishable from Non-being. From pure Being, thus equivalent to Non-being (in the dialect of Hegel), or from God, thus equivalent to Nothing (in that of Erigena), issues that defined existence which is the universe. The world of existence is thus conceived as the self-limitation of the Absolute, the self-analysis of God[3].

The notion of Non-being is further developed by Erigena, in an ingenious fashion, in his five modes of *non esse,* where he distinguishes Being from Non-being, first, in the range of knowledge; second, in the order of things; third, in the process of Nature; fourth, in the mode of apprehension; fifth, in the nature of man. The effect of this scheme is to make the world a complex system of degrees of reality,

[1] Since writing the above I find that Ritter makes the same observation: "Man kann sagen in diesen Unterscheidungen ist die ganze Lehre des Johannes Scotus angelegt, und was er weiter in Besondern von ihr ausführt, ist nur eine Auswendung oder Beschränkung der in ihnen enthaltenen Grundsätze." *Geschichte der Philosophie,* III. p. 220.

[2] Christlieb, *Leben und Lehre des Johannes Scotus Erigena,* p. 130.

[3] Cf. James Ward, *Realm of Ends,* p. 453.

within which every single thing is, from one point of view, real and existent, and from another, unreal and non-existent. Thus, under the second mode, the lower existence is unreal in comparison with the higher existence, right through the universe; under the third mode, all latent existence is unreal in comparison with actual existence; under the fourth mode, all existence known to the senses is unreal in comparison with existence as known to intellect; under the fifth mode, humanity, in its actual state, is unreal in comparison with humanity in its ideal state.

We may not be able to defend all these distinctions, but it is significant that the general conception of degrees of reality has won a prominent place in the most modern range of philosophical ideas. Thus Mr Bradley has written: "The positive relation of every appearance as an adjective to Reality, and the presence of Reality among its appearances in different degrees and with diverse values—this double truth we have found to be the centre of philosophy[1]."

It is difficult to see how any philosophy can maintain the unity and intelligibility of the universe without some such doctrine. Unless the whole of things is a disconnected mass of particulars and therefore not a universe at all, it is impossible to think of every single thing in the mass as on the same plane of reality. The very fact that some things are so ephemeral and others so enduring, that some are so essential and others so negligible in their relation to the rest, would forbid that[2]. It is only reversing the expression of the latter truth to say that the purpose of the whole is more existent and more manifest in some facts of the universe than in others, and that alone constitutes a hierarchy

[1] F. H. Bradley, *Appearance and Reality*, p. 551.
[2] A. S. Pringle-Pattison, *The Idea of God*, p. 220.

of reality. We secure the relative reality of every single fact, and, at the same time, the absolute reality of the universe as a rational system, when we hold the manifold appearances of the world to belong to "successive orders of Reality[1]."

It is in the light of this conception that we must interpret Erigena's statements as to the nothingness of the world of sense[2]. The nothingness of temporal things is relative to the eternal reality of God. The world must be held to be relatively unreal, upon any religious scheme of thought, because it stands contrasted with the absolute reality of God. It is easy enough to speak of Erigena's doctrine as if it meant that the world of sense is sheer illusion, but it is only fair to remember, as a distinguished English philosopher has said, that degrees of illusoriness come to much the same thing as degrees of reality[3]. It is only by some such doctrine, which sees the universe as a graduated scale of reality, that the unity of all existence can be conceived.

And the unity of all being is a necessity of thought. A view of the universe which falls short of such unity merely acquiesces in the failure of thought. Any form of dualism or pluralism is less a philosophy than a substitute for a philosophy. It may indeed be accepted tentatively as the

---

[1] "In the sense that it is the same single experience-system which appears as a whole and in its whole nature in every one of the subordinate experience-systems, they are all alike real, and each is as indispensable as every other to the existence of the whole. In the sense that the whole is more explicitly present in one than in another, there is an infinity of possible degrees of reality and unreality. We should be justified in borrowing a term from mathematical science to mark this double relation of the appearances to their Reality, and speaking of them as successive orders of Reality." A. E. Taylor, *Elements of Metaphysics*, p. 109.

[2] *De Div. Nat.* 561 A.

[3] W. R. Sorley, *Moral Values and the Idea of God*, p. 387.

best working hypothesis, or the best attainable result, but, if so, it is with the instinctive reservation in our minds that if only our knowledge were adequate we should at once be able to pass to a higher view, in which the apparent contradictions of the universe would all be resolved, and we should see *the whole* of existence *as a whole*—that is, as unified by one harmonious purpose. As Lessing said: "῝Εν καὶ πᾶν, that is the whole of philosophy." Any system of thought that denies the unity of the world must ultimately deny the intelligibility of the world. We cannot know things at all unless things are related to each other,—which is simply to say, in other words, that all things are parts of one whole[1].

But while the unity of all being is a necessity of thought, we are not compelled to take the material universe as the whole of being, in the way that the grosser form of pantheism does. That is to express the whole in the lowest terms available, instead of the highest. For the highest form of existence known to us is that of personal life, partially self-conscious, and partially self-determining, and this must necessarily be the basis of the highest conception of existence possible to us, which is that of life at once personal and universal, absolutely self-conscious, and absolutely self-determining, at once cause and effect, at once subject and substance.

It is only in this fashion that we can effectively and worthily conceive of the Absolute. "Erigena, the earliest philosopher of Western Christendom" (as Huber has said), "was the first to express this idea in his system, and his system is not one of Pantheism, but of Theism[2]."

[1] Cf. Edward Caird, *The Evolution of Theology in the Greek Philosophers*, II. p. 80, and Sir Oliver Lodge, *Life and Matter*, p. 10.

[2] Huber, *Johannes Scotus Erigena*, p. 183.

It is scarcely too much to suggest that in this aspect of his philosophy Erigena has approached that view of the Absolute[1] which all idealistic philosophy since Kant has made its particular problem, and which is the special concern, for example, of Hegel and Lotze, and in his own fashion, of Mr F. H. Bradley, in our own land.

There is a remarkable parallel between Erigena and Spinoza in the way that they achieve monism. They both solve the crucial problem of their respective philosophies by a dogmatic assumption. For Spinoza the problem was the opposition of mind and matter, and he reconciled that opposition by his doctrine that thought and extension are not separate things, but different aspects of the same thing, different attributes of one substance.

For Erigena essentially the same problem existed, and he envisaged it as the opposition between God and the world. There is the one, ineffable, immutable superexistence of God, and the manifold and changeable and finite existence of the world as we know it. Erigena resolved this much as Spinoza did his problem by assuming that the opposition is only apparent, and due to the finitude of our minds. For God is the one and only essence of all that is, but He is manifested in all the manifoldness of creation, while remaining still immutable in Himself. So the primal causes are one and indivisible in the Logos, but they are separated as we think of them in our minds and in the world, though still one, and still unchanged in the Logos. So too the substances exist undivided in the primal causes, but they proceed into the diverse actuality of the world, while still remaining in themselves.

All the duality and diversity of the world are on the lower

[1] Huber, *Johannes Scotus Erigena*, p. 179.

side, on the side of material existence and human knowledge. On the higher side, on the side of the eternal and the real, there is absolute unity. In other words, both Erigena and Spinoza attain a monistic doctrine by the assumption that the dualism of the universe is not the real opposition of equally real principles but the apparent duality of one principle, as seen from above and from below, so to speak, *in aeternitate Dei*, and *in temporalitate mundi*.

The difference between them is that Erigena steadily identifies the world of thought with reality and the world of matter with appearance, while in the system of Spinoza the emphasis varies. As Eucken has said: "Spinoza, closely studied, is not a true monist. He alternates between spiritualism and materialism. In the groundwork of his system he is materialistic, and in the conclusion spiritualistic, more particularly in his ethics[1]." The consistent tendency in Erigena is to think of the spiritual aspect as the real side, and of the material aspect as the false one, though the eternal reality is still, in a sense, unknowable. Hence, Erigena's system is much the more genuinely Theistic of the two.

But the greatest difficulty of any system of monism arises not so much from the problem of unity and diversity in the field of existence, as from the moral duality of the world. "Any absolute moralism," as William James once said, "is pluralism: any absolute religion is a monism." That is to say, any philosophy of which the concern is predominantly to maintain the reality of good, and the reality of evil, and therefore the reality of the distinction between them, must emphasise the contradictions of the universe. But any philosophy that is primarily concerned to maintain the

[1] R. Eucken, *Main Currents of Modern Thought*, p. 226.

supremacy of God, and therefore to represent Him as the source and sum of all things, must strive to show that the deep differences that exist in the world are somehow lost in a higher unity.

That is the issue. The demand for unity is intellectual and mystical. The sense of disunity is moral and practical. For any philosophy such as Erigena's, or indeed any religious philosophy that is worth the name, the demand for unity must be supreme; it is impossible to acquiesce in a permanent dualism. As one of the wisest of modern philosophers has said; "God and Evil, in a word, are contraries: if the problem of evil is altogether insoluble, there is an end of Theism: if God exists, there is nothing absolutely evil[1]."

Erigena's doctrine of the non-reality of evil is derived from Augustine[2]. It is found also in Dionysius, and in Maximus (though somewhat modified in the latter by his strong ethical sense), and it goes back to Origen, the Neoplatonists, and perhaps to earlier Oriental mysticism[3]. It has been a favourite tenet with every school of idealist and optimist thought. It is not surprising that it is found in the poets— in George Herbert—

> "Sin is flat opposite the Almighty, seeing
> It wants the good of virtue and of being,"

and in Browning—

> "The evil is null, is naught, is silence implying sound."

It is a doctrine that has been greatly misunderstood, but rightly interpreted, it seems inevitable in any philosophy of

---

[1] James Ward, *Realm of Ends*, p. 319.

[2] *Mali enim nulla natura est; sed amissio boni, malum nomen accipit. De Civ. Dei*, XI. 9. *Peccatum quidem non per ipsum factum est, et manifestum est, quia peccatum nihil est et nihil fiunt homines cum peccant. In Joh. Evang.* I. and a multitude of other passages.

[3] Cf. Tholuck, *Sufismus sive theosophia Persarum pantheistica*, pp. 254-5.

religion. It should be remembered that it is the doctrine of Origen[1] and John of Damascus[2], of Anselm[3] and Thomas Aquinas[4], as well as of Erigena and Augustine.

It does not mean that evil simply does not exist. No sane man has ever denied the actual existence of evil in the world. Evil, as a phenomenon, is as real as anything else in this world of phenomena. Hence any scheme of thought, such as materialism or positivism, which accepts no reality beyond the phenomenal, could not possibly tolerate or even understand any doctrine of the non-reality of evil. But theism, or indeed idealism of any kind, *must* hold evil to be unreal, in some sense. For the fundamental postulate of any theistic or idealistic doctrine is a reality beyond the world of phenomena, a reality which (because it is a primary and an ultimate reality) is more real than the phenomenal reality; an *omnitudo realitatis*, an absolute reality, in comparison with which phenomenal reality is relatively unreal. If God is the primal, the eternal, the unoriginated Reality, then all that begins and ends, all that once was not, and once again will not be, all that derives a momentary reality from God, and is de-

---

[1] πάντες μὲν οὖν οἱ μετέχοντες τοῦ Ὄντος, μετέχουσι δὲ οἱ ἅγιοι, εὐλόγως ἂν Ὄντες χρηματίζοιεν· οἱ δὲ ἀποστραφέντες τὴν τοῦ Ὄντος μετοχήν, τῷ ἐστερῆσθαι τοῦ Ὄντος γεγόνασιν Οὐκ ὄντες....καὶ πᾶσα ἡ κακία Οὐδέν ἐστιν ἐπεὶ καὶ Οὐκ ὂν τυγχάνει. *Comm. in Evang. Joh.* II. 13 (7). (The reference is to the οὐδέν in John i. 3.) Cf. *De Princ.* II. 9.

[2] ἡ γὰρ κακία οὐδὲν ἕτερόν ἐστιν, εἰ μὴ ἀναχώρησις τοῦ ἀγαθοῦ. *De Fide Orth.* II. 30.

[3] *Malum non est aliud, quam non bonum, aut absentia boni, ubi debet et expedit esse bonum. De Casu Diaboli,* X. *Hac ipsa ratione intelligimus malum nihil esse. Sicut enim injustitia non est aliud, quam absentia debitae justitiae: ita malum non est aliud, quam absentia debiti boni. De Conceptu Virginali et Originali Peccato,* V.

[4] *Malum enim est defectus boni quod natum est et debet haberi. Summ. Theol.* Pt. I. qu. 49, art. I. Cf. Thomas Harper, S.J., *Metaphysics of the School,* I. pp. 574-5.

pendent upon His will and His act for its very existence, —all this is unreal, in comparison with His reality, Who is the *Ens realissimum*.

But if this is true of all derived and temporal existence, it is doubly true of the existence of evil. For the good not only exists phenomenally, but it exists in immediate derivation from God, Who is the ultimate good and the ultimate reality, and it exists because it eternally ought to exist; but the evil only exists phenomenally and cannot be derived from or dependent on God, and ought not to exist at all, and is therefore, by the terms of its existence, the very opposite, the utter contradiction, of eternal and ultimate reality. In this sense it must be said to be unreal[1].

Erigena teaches that evil, as negative, is causeless[2]. It is useless to seek for a cause of evil, for what is mere absence of good, mere privation of existence, cannot have a cause. It arises from the irrational motion of the will, and so the will is, in a sense, the source of it, as the sphere in which it arises, but it is strictly uncaused. This, like the rest of Erigena's theory of evil, is expressly from Augustine[3].

---

[1] "Good is not merely that which is, but that which ought to be: not reality alone, but necessity also belongs to it. Evil, on the contrary, while possessing an empirical existence, is that which ought not to be; it exists only as an infringement of, or opposition to, an ideal law." Müller, *Christian Doctrine of Sin*, I. p. 193.

[2] This is also the doctrine of Spinoza who treats evil as "an illusion of relativity." As such it is causeless. "It is idle to trouble ourselves about the cause of Sin; for Sin is non-being and non-being wants no cause." Martineau, *A Study of Spinoza*, p. 263.

[3] "If the further question be asked, What was the efficient cause of the evil will? there is none....Let no one, therefore, look for an efficient cause of the evil will; for it is not efficient, but deficient, as the will itself is not an effecting of something but a defect....Now to seek to discover the causes of these defections (causes, as I have said, not efficient but deficient), is as if some one sought to see darkness or to hear silence." *De Civ. Dei*, XII. 6. 7.

Erigena's doctrine of the negativity of evil must not blind us to the fact that he recognises evil as a real, positive, and militant power. There are many passages which illustrate this. It is easy to regard this as mere inconsistency. Perhaps it is finally inconsistent in a logical sense, but that is arguable, for the two positions are not on the same plane. An ultimate metaphysical doctrine is not to be regarded as an immediate conclusion for practical life. We may deny the doctrine of the older natural philosophy, as to the extension and solidity of matter, and hold that these attributes may be resolved into an arrangement of electrical force, but that does not mean that you will not break your head if you collide with a stone wall. Erigena never dreamt of denying the present phenomenal reality of evil. He was only concerned to deny that it is an ultimate constituent of the universe, one of those essential and eternal realities that are, in his view of existence, the only realities.

It may be noted here that there is an inconsistency between Erigena's doctrine that the Holy Spirit is the cause of the distribution and division of all individual existence, and his doctrine that evil is the source of all division. We should expect him to mean that the Spirit is the source of natural differentiation and that evil is the source of unnatural severance, but he does not make this distinction. On the contrary, he expressly states that differences and divisions of quantity, quality, time, space, and so forth, are all due to sin[1]. And the reunion of the redeemed creation in Christ is not described as merely the reunion of the divisions directly consequent upon human sin, such as the distinction of sex, but as the reunion of all the manifold individuality of the

[1] *De Div. Nat.* 533 B.

creation in the superessential unity of God, though individuality is not lost in God.

All this is in manifest conflict with other express statements that the Holy Spirit is the cause of the distribution and division of all that the Father creates in the Son,—the distribution of causes in their effects, and the division of these in genera, species, and number[1].

It has been argued that Erigena absolutely denies the doctrine of Original Sin, by his theory that evil is not implanted in human nature[2]. This is scarcely fair to our philosopher. Erigena more than once expressly speaks of the guilt of Original Sin as remitted in Baptism[3]. It is clear enough therefore that he believed himself to hold the orthodox doctrine. The most that can be fairly urged against this is that upon two points (in both of which he depended upon Augustine) he held it in a somewhat special form. He held, in the first place, that the primal sin was not so much the sin of an individual as the transgression of humanity; it was man, rather than a man, that sinned in Adam. *Non enim primus Adam ille, qui ex generalitate naturae humanae ante ceteros in mundum hunc visibilem venit, solus peccavit, sed omnes peccaverunt, priusquam in mundum procederent. Nam quod Apostolus ait, sicut enim in Adam omnes moriuntur, ita in Christo omnes vivificantur, non de ipso uno ac primo homine intelligimus, sed nomine Adam omnem generaliter naturam humanam significari accipimus[4].* And, in the second

---

[1] *De Div. Nat.* 566 A, B.

[2] Christlieb, *Leben und Lehre des Johannes Scotus Erigena*, p. 318.

[3] *De Div. Nat.* 847 A. *Comm. in Evang. sec. Joan.* 310 C.

[4] *Comm. in Evang. sec. Joan.* 310 D. It was the doctrine of Augustine that all sinned in Adam, since all were in him, and, in a sense, all *were* that one man. *In Adam totum genus humanum radicaliter institutum est.* (*De Genesi*, VI. 14.) *Ipsum esse totum genus humanum.* (*In Johannis Ev. Tract.* X. 11.) *Omnes*

place, he denied that evil was implanted in human *nature*, not that he was at all concerned to deny the internal corruption of humanity, but because it was vital to his system that evil was rooted in the human *will*. *Non in humana natura plantatum est malum, sed in perverso et irrationabili motu rationabilis liberaeque voluntatis est constitutum*[1]. *Peccata non naturalia sunt, sed voluntaria*[2]. Erigena held that the nature—the essential nature—of every being, even of the demons, is good, incorruptible and immortal, as derived from God and dependent upon Him. All evil therefore, whether in angels or in man, all sin, whether original or actual, is rooted not in the essential nature, but in a perverse motion of the free will[3].

Erigena's doctrine of evil, in this respect as in all others, is closely connected with his theory of being, as that is again with his theory of knowledge. Evil cannot exist in

fuimus in illo uno, quomodo omnes fuimus ille unus. (*De Civ. Dei*, XIII. 3. 14.) This really goes back to the Vulgate mistranslation of Rom. v. 12, "Wherefore as by one man sin entered into the world, and death by sin; and so death passed upon all men, *for that* all have sinned," ἐφ' ᾧ πάντες ἥμαρτον, which was rendered, *in quo omnes peccaverunt*, "*in whom* all have sinned" (taking ἐφ' ᾧ as equivalent to ἐν ᾧ). *Ab Adam, in quo omnes peccavimus, non omnia nostra peccata, sed tantum originale traduximus, a Christo vero, in quo omnes justificamur, non illius tantum originalis, sed etiam ceterorum, quae ipsi addidimus, peccatorum remissionem consequimur.* (*De Peccat. Merit.* I. 14. 16.) Compare *De Trin.* IV. 12. Gregory of Nyssa also teaches that Adam is humanity. *De Hominis Opificio* (185 B, Vol. 44, ed. Migne).

[1] *De Div. Nat.* 828 D.

[2] *Ibid.* 944 A.

[3] "No nature whatever is evil, and the name belongs only to the privation of good." *De Civ. Dei*, II. 22. "Things solely good, therefore, can in some circumstances exist: things solely evil, never, for even those natures which are vitiated by an evil will, so far indeed as they are vitiated, are evil, but in so far as they are natures they are good." *De Civ. Dei*, XII. 3. "Evil is not from (*ex*) God, nor coeternal with God, but evil arose out of the free will of our rational nature, which was created good by Him Who is good." *Op. imp. c. Julian.* VI. 5. See also *Conf.* VII. 2, *Enchir.* 23, and many other passages.

any nature, for every nature exists in immediate dependence upon God, since it owes its existence to the knowledge of God.

Nowhere does Erigena's idealism appear more clearly than in this region. The idea of things in the mind of God is the essence of the things[1]. God does not know them because they are, but they are, because God knows them. And, as all that God knows is because He knows it, so all sensible and intelligible things that the mind of man can know exist, in a secondary sense, because man knows them. Their essential and eternal existence derives from the knowledge of God : their actual existence in the world of space and time depends upon the knowledge of man. Not the mere knowledge of perception, that is, but the innate knowledge which exists in the mind of man because all things were created in the nature of man. Man is literally a microcosm: the whole creation exists ideally in humanity; it was created in man, and it is to be redeemed and restored to unity in man. The reason of man is all that it knows, as effect, as the Divine Reason is all that it knows, as cause. And, as the idea of things is the substance of things, it follows that the whole of the lower creation exists more truly in the mind of man than it exists in itself[2]. This thought, like so much else, Erigena borrowed from Augustine[3].

[1] This is expressly from Augustine. *Universas autem creaturas suas, et spiritales et corporales, non quia sunt, ideo novit ; sed ideo sunt quia novit. Non enim nescivit quae fuerat creaturus. Quia ergo scivit, creavit ; non quia creavit, scivit. De Trin.* XV. 13. It is also the doctrine of Thomas Aquinas. *Scientia Dei est causa rerum. Sic enim scientia Dei se habet ad omnes res creatas, sicut scientia artificis se habet artificiata. Scientia autem artificis est causa artificiatorum ; eo quod artifex operatur per suum intellectum. Unde oportet quod forma intellectus sit principium operationis ; sicut calor est principium calefactionis. Summ. Theol.* I. qu. 14, art. 8.

[2] Huber, *Johannes Scotus Erigena*, pp. 312–315.

[3] "When we speak of bodies by means of bodily sense, there arises in our mind some likeness of them, which is a phantasm of the memory; for the

The idealism of Erigena stands in a singular relation at this point to the philosophies of the past and of the present. There are only two great types of idealist thought—the Platonic, which was the source of all ancient and mediaeval idealism, and the Berkeleyan, which determined the character of all modern idealism. The one makes the *nexus* of being and knowledge a system of creative ideas, an order of hypostasised universals. The other makes it a system of creative minds, an order of conscious centres[1]. The one therefore postulates three centres of existence as known,— the mind of God[2], the "ideas," the mind of man; whereas the other only needs two, eliminating the whole doctrine of ideas. Erigena uses all three conceptions, God, the *causae primordiales*, and the human mind. But he needs only the first and the last term. The primal causes, which are his version of the Platonic ideas, are really in this respect an excrescence in his system. He definitely teaches, as we have seen, that the knowledge of things in the mind of God is the essence of the things, *causaliter*, and that the knowledge of them in the mind of man is the essence of them *effectualiter*. That being so, he has an idealist structure of the universe complete to his hand. Nothing more is needed than that God should think the world into universal exist-

bodies themselves are not at all in the mind, when we think them, but only the likenesses of those bodies; therefore, when we approve the latter for the former, we err, for the approving of one thing for another is an error; yet the image of the body in the mind is a thing of a better sort than the species of the body itself, inasmuch as the former is in a better nature, viz. in a living existence, as the mind is." *De Trin.* XI. 2.

[1] J. S. Mackenzie, *Elements of Constructive Philosophy*, pp. 140–1. A. S. Pringle-Pattison, *The Idea of God*, p. 376.

[2] From the point of view of the above paragraph the character of Plato's theism does not matter. The Form of the Good—ἡ τοῦ ἀγαθοῦ ἰδέα—as the supreme universal, is at least a metaphysical equivalent of the notion of Deity.

ence, and that each man should think his partial world into existence, in ultimate dependence upon the thought of God. Erigena, in fact, had thought his way to the standpoint of Berkeley, but he could not cut himself adrift from the doctrine of ideas developed by the Neoplatonists as he found it in the pseudo-Dionysius. He retained it, as he retained the notion of formless matter, in deference to philosophic and patristic authority, when he did not really need it. It makes his system needlessly complex, and it prevented him from completely forestalling the modern systems of idealism.

While the conception of knowledge as innate in man is maintained, Erigena admits that all the material of knowledge comes to us through the bodily senses. But these could only present us with a multitude of unrelated sensations, a manifold of experience, if there were not reason within us, which gives unity and intelligibility to the mass of sensations[1]. It would be impossible to have a true knowledge of sensible things, if we had only the senses to give it. It is reason that makes the sensible world that we apprehend intelligible, and that makes it one[2].

But Erigena's theory of knowledge is not consistent. There are other passages in which the soul is represented, in the act of knowledge, as an essential trinity of νοῦς, λόγος,

---

[1] De Div. Nat. 868 D.

[2] Das Material zu diesen Operationen des Denkens kann uns immer nur durch die körperlichen Sinne geboten werden aber diese vermögen für sich allein doch nur eine schlechthinnige Vielheit von Bildern der im Wechsel begriffenen Erscheinungen zu liefern: die Sinnlichkeit würde somit unmittelbar für sich allein an der flüchtigen Erscheinung haften käme daher nie dazu eine wahre Erkenntniss der Dinge zu gewinnen. Nur mit Hülfe der Vernunft oder des Geistes ist es möglich, die Einheit des Mannigfaltigen, den Begriff zu erfassen. Kaulich, Entwicklung der scholastischen Philosophie von Johannes Scotus Erigena bis Abälard, p. 109.

διάνοια, a threefold movement of the soul (this is borrowed from Dionysius) around God, and the primordial causes, and the effects of those causes. When the human soul knows God, it is *intellectus*; when it knows the primal causes, it is *ratio*; when it knows the world of appearances, it is *sensus interior*. In each case the act of knowledge is conceived as a motion (*motus*) of the soul around the object of knowledge—a sort of contact with the thing known. It is obvious that this is a very different conception of knowledge from that which holds man to be a microcosm, carrying the whole universe ideally within himself[1].

It was urged by Baur[2] (and the criticism was repeated by Christlieb)[3] that Erigena cannot legitimately come by the conception of *intellectus*, since God, in His absolute identity and infinitude, cannot be conceived as self-conscious Thought. And, if so, whence comes thought at all? Notwithstanding the great name of Baur, and the greater name of Kant, from whom the idea really comes, the criticism is a shallow one. It amounts to this, that because the antithesis of subject and object, *ego* and *non-ego*, which is found in all human thought, is unthinkable as applied to God, therefore there cannot be the reality of thought or self-consciousness in God. Stated in that way, the objection is seen to be merely anthropomorphism *in excelsis*. It is moreover defective psychology. It is the peculiarity of self-consciousness, as has been well said, "that it is no simple unity or identity; for if so, it must be purely an object, or purely a subject, but really it is both in one; all other things are for it, but it is *for itself*. If knowledge is the relation

---

[1] Huber, *Johannes Scotus Erigena*, p. 340.
[2] Baur, *Lehre v. d. Dreieinigkeit*, II. p. 284.
[3] Christlieb, *Leben und Lehre des Johannes Scotus Erigena*, p. 203.

of an object to a conscious subject, it is the more complete, the more intimate the relation; and it becomes perfect when the duality becomes transparent, when subject and object are identified, and when the duality is seen to be simply the necessary expression of the unity—in short, when consciousness passes into self-consciousness[1]." When once that essential characteristic of self-consciousness is understood, it follows that the only perfect knowledge, and the only perfect personality, must be where all is at once subject and object, and must belong to "One for Whom there is no essential not-self, because all essential experience is His own; an infinite fulness or Pleroma, in the language of St Paul[2]."

The *cogito ergo sum* of Descartes, which is the point of departure of all modern philosophy[3], is clearly anticipated by Erigena in a very remarkable passage[4]. The anticipation is formal, for the Scot makes the express point that consciousness is the warranty of existence; whether I know, or whether I know not, whether I am assured of my own

---

[1] Edward Caird, *Hegel*, p. 147.

[2] J. R. Illingworth, *Divine Transcendence*, p. 21.

[3] "When Descartes took his *cogito ergo sum* as alone certain, and provisionally regarded the existence of the world as problematical, he really discovered the essential and only right starting-point of all philosophy, and at the same time its true foundation. This foundation is essentially and inevitably the subjective, the individual consciousness. For this alone is and remains immediate; everything else, whatever it may be, is mediated and conditioned through it, and is therefore dependent upon it." Schopenhauer, *The World as Will and Idea*, i. i.

[4] *Scio enim me esse, nec tamen me praecedit scientia mei, quia non aliud sum, et aliud scientia, qua me scio; et si nescirem me esse, non nescirem ignorare me esse; ac per hoc, sive scivero, sive nescivero me esse, scientia non carebo; mihi enim remanebit scire ignorantiam meam. Et si omne, quod potest scire se ipsum nescire, non potest ignorare se ipsum esse; nam si penitus non esset, non sciret seipsum nescire: conficitur omnino esse omne, quod scit se esse, vel scit se nescire se esse. De Div. Nat. 776 B.*

existence, or whether I doubt it, it is still I that know, or I that know not, still I that believe, or I that doubt, still I that think, whether my thought is true or false ; and therefore I am. But Erigena borrowed the thought, as he did so much else, from Augustine[1]. It is set forth in one of the most striking passages that Augustine ever wrote.

There is one thought in Erigena's work, to which he often recurs, that might have been a valuable element in his philosophy, but it is never really worked out. It is the notion of a vision of the truth, more immediate and more final than any formal knowledge can give. This *gnostica virtus*[2], *gnostica scientia*[3] (the phrase is borrowed from Maximus), or *intellectualis visio*[4], evidently means a spiritual intuition in which the soul passes beyond itself, and reaches an unmediated apprehension of the Absolute[5]. It reminds us of the *intellectuelle Anschauung* of Schelling and Hegel, the standpoint of the Absolute Idea, from which all differences, discords and parts are seen to disappear. It is closely parallel, also, to Spinoza's third mode of knowledge[6]— *scientia intuitiva*, that adequate knowledge in which lies the

---

[1] "I am not at all afraid of the arguments of the Academicians, who say, What if you are deceived? For if I am deceived, I am. For he who is not, cannot be deceived; and if I am deceived, by this same token I am. And since I am if I am deceived, how am I deceived in believing that I am? for it is certain that I am if I am deceived. Since, therefore, I, the person deceived, should be, even if I were deceived, certainly I am not deceived in this knowledge that I am. And, consequently, neither am I deceived in knowing that I know. For as I know that I am, so I know this also, that I know." *De Civ. Dei*, XI. 26. (Cf. also *De Trin.* X. 14.)

[2] *De Div. Nat.* 670 B.

[3] *Ibid.* 535 A. γνωστικὴ θεωρία, Maximus, *Ambigua*, 1297 A (Vol. 91, ed. Migne).

[4] *De Praed.* 368 B.

[5] Erdmann, *History of Philosophy*, I. p. 294.

[6] Spinoza, *Ethics*, II. 40. 2.

unity of the knowledge of the universal and of the knowledge of the individual[1].

But there is little more in Erigena than the suggestion that is involved in the recurrent phrases. He never elaborates any real doctrine of intuition, in this sense.

Every modern reader must feel that one of the greatest defects of Erigena's philosophic system is that it is of so purely intellectual a texture. The student, as he works through the Scot's dialectics, is inclined to be more than impatient with him for what Mr Schiller criticised in Mr Bradley (in a devastating phrase) as his "inhuman, incompetent and impracticable intellectualism[2]." But it is scarcely fair to condemn or even to criticise our mediaeval philosopher for that fault. The criticism applies more or less to all philosophies of the past[3]. It often seems as if philosophy were beating about in endless circles from age to age, in perpetually considering afresh the same ultimate problems. The circles, however, are really spirals: there is an upward progress, for there is an advance in the treatment of the problems even if the problems are insoluble. Perhaps the most unchallenged advance of philosophy during the last generation or two has been precisely this, that while in

[1] Christlieb, *Leben und Lehre des Johannes Scotus Erigena*, pp. 149–156.

[2] *Personal Idealism*, p. 127.

[3] "The philosophies of Plato and Aristotle, which have determined the main trend of all subsequent speculation till comparatively recent times, shew a marked bias toward what is nowadays called Intellectualism. According to this, cognition is the primary factor in experience....What is called Voluntarism, however, inverts all this. Conation, not cognition, is regarded as fundamental to life: it is the blind impulse to live that leads on to knowledge, just as it is for the sake of life that knowledge is valued; and not *vice versa*. This doctrine of the primary fact of the practical, first definitely announced by Kant, repeated and extended by Fichte, was still more emphatically proclaimed by Schopenhauer." James Ward, *The Realm of Ends*, p. 198.

the past all the problems have been envisaged from the point of view of intellect alone, they are now seen in relation to life and action, will and emotion. This is the natural result of modern psychological research. Consciousness is realised to be more than cognition, and, on the larger scale, life is seen to be larger than logic. A purely intellectual solution of the enigma of the universe, even if it were possible, would now be felt to be inadequate[1]. But to Erigena, as to all the philosophers of the past, all the ultimate problems were intellectual problems, and the only conceivable solution was an intellectual solution.

Erigena has no real definitions of either will or feeling. He vindicates the freedom of the will very thoroughly, but he does not attempt to say anywhere what the will is. There is no psychological analysis of will, and indeed we do not expect to find it in the ninth century. The will is always represented from the standpoint of moral choice. It is the will that chooses between good and evil, between that knowledge of God which is eternal blessedness, and that delight in the delusive things of this world which is the principle of sin. There is nowhere in Erigena's writings, we think, any reference to the human will which has not primarily this ethical sense.

With regard to feeling Erigena is more rudimentary still. He has nowhere any reference to feeling, as a definite and distinguishable element in human experience. It is never mentioned, except in the sense of sensation[2].

Erigena always makes the knowledge of God and the experience of redemption consist in intellectual contem-

[1] "No solution of the problem of God and man can be reached from a consideration of man as a merely cognitive being." A. S. Pringle-Pattison, *The Idea of God*, p. 291. Cf. Eucken, *Main Currents of Modern Thought*, p. 225.

[2] Huber, *Johannes Scotus Erigena*, p. 337.

plation. *In quantum quippe quisque cogitationi veritatis appropinquabit in tantum rapietur obviam Christo in aëra, hoc est, in purissimae intelligentiae altitudinem et claritatem, ac sic semper in nube contemplationis suae in divinis theophaniis et erit et gaudebit*[1]. The whole of the facts of religion are regarded much too exclusively from this intellectual standpoint[2].

It is the principle of love that Erigena neglects. In the religious sense this is the greatest defect of his scheme of thought. The love of God is never definitely conceived in his system of the universe, except as the attraction by which all things in the world are drawn back into God, in a returning cycle. How far this falls short of the essential thought of Christianity—the thought of a love which is at once personal and universal, and which, by a personal sacrifice, achieves a universal redemption—it is scarcely necessary to show in any detail. A conception of the love of God which makes it a sort of universal magnetism, or at the best a boundless desire, is far removed from that which says, *God so loved the world that He gave His Son, the only begotten!*

The doctrine of *adunatio* is the climax of Erigena's philosophy, as it must be of any philosophy that works within the sphere of Christianity. It is conceived as the completion of a cycle. The waxing and waning moon, the circling stars, the ebbing and flowing tides, the growth and decay of all living creatures, are all examples of this universal principle of return. As in the material world, so it is in the world of the intellect. The science of numbers begins with the monad,

---

[1] *De Div. Nat.* 998 c.
[2] Christlieb, *Leben und Lehre des Johannes Scotus Erigena*, p. 415. Cf. W. R. Inge, *Christian Mysticism*, p. 133.

and always seeks to regain it. The art of dialectic begins with the most general notion of being, and always strives to revert to it. Thus all things illustrate the principle that existence is a great cycle, which begins from God and returns to God. As the Fall of man began all the divisions and oppositions of the universe, so the return of man to God will resolve and reconcile them all. Man is the centre of union in the process of creation ; man is the source of division through sin; man is the centre of reunion in the process of redemption.

Perhaps the greatest defect of all this conception of *adunatio* lies in this very fact that the whole existence of the universe is conceived as a mere cycle beginning from the superessential existence of God, and returning to it. While that conception is maintained (however difficult it may be to escape from it) it seems to be impossible to retain the reality of the temporal universe in any satisfying sense. For when all has been reabsorbed into the Absolute, what has the cosmic process accomplished ? What is different because anything did ever exist ? What has been achieved by the immense structure of the creation, by all the labour and experience and suffering of humanity ?

It is true that Erigena strives to save the individuality of things, when all has returned into the unity of the Absolute. But he does not go on to show (and with his Neoplatonist conception of God, he could not) that the Divine Nature is actually enriched by the absorption of all that is reunited with it. A daring thought like that would at least help us to conceive that the secular processes of the world, and all the struggles of mankind, had some real significance and some eternal value. But Erigena never really develops this thought. The nearest that he approaches to it is when, following Origen and Augustine, he argues that, without a creation, God would be only the possible Creator, only the potential Lord of all. This means that the creation is necessary to the Divine Nature, and indeed Erigena goes as far as that, but this again, if it means anything, means that in some inconceivable way the being of God is enriched by the primal emanation from Him and by the final return to Him of all that is, and to this point our philosopher never definitely advances. Such a conception is finely hinted by Schiller:

> "Freundlos war der grosse Weltenmeister,
> Fühlte Mangel—darum schuf er Geister,
>   Sel'ge Spiegel seiner Seligkeit!
> Fand das höchste Wesen schon kein Gleiches,
> Aus dem Kelch des ganzen Seelenreiches
>   Schäumt ihm—die Unendlichkeit."

It seems to be only in some such way that the existence of the universe can be justified in the last review. The conception is difficult enough from the point of view of the metaphysics of religion, for how can we think of God as lacking any possible experience, when the very character of the Divine existence is that of a $\pi\lambda\acute{\eta}\rho\omega\mu\alpha$? Yet it seems impossible, unless the life of the universe means something which we can only express crudely as a new experience in the life of the Deity, to see in the end of all any result that is

> "worth
> This pomp of worlds, this pain of birth."

This conception is philosophically difficult, because philosophy thinks of God as the Absolute, but it is not so difficult from the purely religious standpoint. Indeed, it may be said to be inevitable, in that sense. For if orthodox Christianity means anything, it means that God became man, and redeemed man by the death of the Cross, and that fact (as John of Damascus once splendidly said) is "a new thing, the newest of all new things, the only really new thing under the sun[1]." The fact of redemption is the central fact of the universe, and it is a new event in the history of God. There is doubtless a sense in which it dates from eternity—τὸ ἀρνίον ἐσφαγμένον ἀπὸ καταβολῆς κόσμου— the eternal Love was always in essence a redeeming Love. But the act of redemption was in time, and unless, like the Docetae, we are to reduce the whole earthly life of Christ to a mere masque, we must regard it as a new fact in the life of God, and, in that sense, if it may be reverently said, as an enrichment of the Divine experience.

The philosophic principle of which Erigena makes most use in all this region is one of much interest and much value. It bulks largely in the system of Hegel[2]. Briefly, it is this, that the higher existence does not destroy and deny the lower existence, but absorbs and affirms it, so that the lower really exists more truly in its union with the higher than in its own right. All things that have ever had an existence derived from God—all things, that is, with the exception of what is evil, which never does really exist— will exist more truly in God, when God is all in all, than they ever existed in themselves. It is only phenomenally that anything ceases to be. Essentially and eternally, it exists in God; it exists in Him as truly as ever it existed, more truly than ever it existed in this world of shadows. This is the faith which confronts us in those astonishing lines of Emily Brontë:

---

[1] *De Fide Orth.* III. I.
[2] Cf. A. S. Pringle-Pattison, *Hegelianism and Personality*, p. 201.

"Though earth and man were gone,
    And suns and universes ceased to be,
And Thou wert left alone,
    Every existence would exist in Thee.

"There is not room for Death
    Nor atom that his might could render void,
Thou, Thou art Being and Breath,
    And what Thou art may never be destroyed."

It is at any rate a fruitful thought, and one which has much warrant in the actual structure of the world, that lower ranges of being are at once included in and transcended by the higher ranges, "as animal life transcends and yet includes chemical activity; while human personality again transcends and includes animal life[1]." There can be no doubt that this is a genuine characteristic of existence, —one of the structural principles of the universe. As a distinguished modern thinker has said: "it is everywhere the mark of the higher and wider experience to comprehend the lower and narrower, whereas the contrary is excluded by the very nature of the case[2]." According to Erigena's thought, nothing is lost, nothing is reduced; rather everything has a more perfect existence in the nature of God than it ever had in the world of time and sense. There is no effacement of personality; angels and men will exist in God without ceasing to be themselves. There will be "an infinite number of *foci* in one infinite consciousness[3]."

It is inevitable that this doctrine of *adunatio* should be the least satisfactory part of Erigena's scheme of thought. It is attempting the formal construction of what is really inconceivable, except in the way of mystical suggestion and

[1] J. R. Illingworth, *Divine Transcendence*, p. 17.
[2] A. S. Pringle-Pattison, *The Idea of God*, p. 365.
[3] W. R. Inge, *The Philosophy of Plotinus*, I. p. 216.

religious intuition. There is something pathetically naïve
in Erigena's careful construction of a deliberate scheme of
ἀποκατάστασις, with numbered stages and elaborate details,
when the whole region is one absolutely unknown to human
experience and almost unapproachable to human thought,
and when we have nothing whatever to proceed upon but a
few hints in Scripture, and a deep longing of the Christian
soul. These last may warrant an inexpressible hope, but
they certainly cannot warrant more.

The greatest difficulty that Erigena consciously encounters
in this region is the reconciliation of the opposite doctrines
that evil finally ceases to be, and that the punishment of
evil is eternal. He seeks to effect the reconciliation by his
principle that evil does not exist in any created nature, but
only in the irrational motion of the will, and that therefore
no created nature will be punished. The unnatural desire
of the will which constitutes evil will be punished, and
punished eternally[1], if it persists eternally, by its own eternal
futility, and by its remorse for the past, but as this, like all
evil, is causeless and unreal, it is possible to present the
conception of a future where every thing that really exists
is reconciled to God. No one can help feeling that this is a
mere trick of dialectic. If there is evil desire at all, or the
remembrance of it, in however meagre a sense, if it is only
the mere absence of a blessedness that might have been,
still there is a shadow in that world of light, and what is
evil has not wholly vanished from the restored universe.
There is no escape from this dilemma.

[1] *Non autem hoc dicimus, quasi nulla poena sit aeterna, dum unusquisque
sua conscientia sive beatificabitur, sive damnabitur in aeternum, sed solummodo
agimus, quod nulla natura in ullo punietur. Expos. super Ierarchiam Caelestem
S. Dionysii,* 204 D–205 A.

In this section of his system Erigena also uses the thought, borrowed from Augustine[1], that evil, which is seen as defect and deformity in our partial view of the universe, is resolved into an element of universal beauty as seen in the whole of existence. He quotes Augustine's image of the black shadow, ugly in itself, but helping to create the beauty of the picture. True reason does not hesitate to declare, he says, that what is evil, misery, retribution, as seen in a part of the universe, is not evil, not misery, not retribution, as seen in the whole. Hell itself is good, as a part of the ordered beauty of the whole universe. "All discord, harmony not understood; All partial evil, universal good."

It is hardly necessary to point out that this is inconsistent with Erigena's main contention that evil is essentially unreal. He seems, in this part of his system, to grasp at any and every thought that promises to dispose of evil, without pausing to consider their mutual inconsistency. He wavers between two ultimate positions that are entirely irreconcilable[2]. One is that even as an illusory appearance evil finally disappears, since it never had any real existence at all—which is his essential doctrine throughout. The other is that evil is finally discerned to be not evil but good, when all things are seen in the perspective of eternity. But on

---

[1] "And to Thee is nothing whatsoever evil; yea, not only to Thee, but also to Thy creation as a whole, because there is nothing without, which may break in, and corrupt that order which Thou hast appointed it. But in the parts thereof some things, because unharmonising with other some, are accounted evil; whereas those very things harmonise with others and are good; and in themselves are good." *Conf.* VII. 13.

[2] There is a similar inconsistency in the system of Plotinus. "In this attempt to explain, or explain away, evil, we see Plotinus wavering between a iustification of it as a necessary means to a greater good, and the denial of its reality except as a transient appearance of the phenomenal world." Edward Caird, *The Evolution of Theology in the Greek Philosophers*, II. p. 335.

Erigena's own principles, how can evil, which is unreal, ever be, or appear to be, good, which is the final reality?

A great deal of this doctrine as to the non-perpetuity of evil Erigena borrowed directly from Gregory of Nyssa. There he found his splendid metaphor of the shadow of the earth, projected into space, which we call night, diminishing into nothingness, and finally absorbed into the encircling light of the sun that fills the universe.

This is the climax of Erigena's thought, as it must be of all thought that moves within the large sphere of the Christian faith and rises to the sublime height of the Christian hope. We are left gazing over "the dizzy verge, the dazzling line, Where mortal and immortal merge, And human dies divine." All is good, and all is one, for God is all in all. "With this conception[1]" (as the best of all the expositors of Erigena has written) "where the gaze is no longer fixed upon individual existences, but has widened to a view of the whole universe, the spirit is no longer at the standpoint of human knowledge, but has risen to the height of the Divine outlook, where, as Novalis beautifully says, there are no more clouds, but all is one brightness."

[1] Huber, *Johannes Scotus Erigena*, p. 428.

IV. SOURCES AND AUTHORITIES

IT may be surprising to those who have regarded Erigena as more of a philosopher than of a theologian, and as exalting reason at the expense of authority, to find that his constant appeal is to the Scriptures. It is true that he declares reason to be greater than authority, since reason is prior to nature, and authority belongs to time; since, moreover, authority proceeds from reason, for it is nothing else but the strength of reason in the Fathers discovering the truth, and then commending it to posterity. But he also declares that reason and authority are not to be opposed, for right reason and true authority must always agree[1].

It is a quaint misunderstanding to write as if Erigena were a modern rationalist, in whose mind reason and authority were perpetually opposed. His whole position is that of Augustine, that authority is simply the established result of reason, reason being prior in essence to authority[2]. All authority goes back to the rationality of the universe; right authority therefore must agree with right reason. There cannot be a schism between them: if there appears to be one, it can only be that in that particular case authority is false, or reason is wrong, which is simply to say that the authority is no authority or that the reason is no reason.

[1] *De Div. Nat.* 513 C. "Mais si elle [la pensée de Scot Érigène] n'est orthodoxe de fait, elle l'est d'intention et ne conçoit pas la possibilité d'opposer, ni même de séparer, la foi et la raison. Si l'autorité sur laquelle on s'appuie est vraie et si la raison pense juste, elles ne sauraient se contredire, parce que l'autorité vraie et la droite raison découlent d'une même source qui est la sagesse divine." E. Gilson, *La Philosophie au Moyen Age*, I. p. 14.
[2] *De Ord.* II. 9 (26).

Erigena defers to the opinions of the Fathers, but he frankly accepts the Scripture as his final authority[1], and displays a most extensive knowledge of it accordingly. There are more than three hundred and fifty distinct quotations from the Bible in *The Division of Nature* alone[2], and they range over most of the books of the canon. Every book in the New Testament is quoted, except four of the smaller Epistles.

There is nothing whatever to show any acquaintance with the original text of the Old Testament. It was indeed suggested by Guizot and Hegel[3] (following Hjort) that Erigena knew Hebrew. But practically the sole evidence for this is the fact that in quoting Genesis i. 2 he criticises the rendering of the LXX, ἀόρατος καὶ ἀκατασκεύαστος, *invisibilis et incomposita*, and states that the Vulgate reading, *inanis et vacua*[4], is the right rendering of the Hebrew. This he had probably learned from Jerome, along with several etymologies of Hebrew proper names. He fails to correct other passages where both the LXX and the Vulgate misrepresent the Hebrew. His ignorance of Hebrew is perhaps sufficiently proved by the fact that he actually quotes the authority of Jerome on the very elementary detail that names ending in -*im*, like cherubim, signify the masculine plural (865 B). He quotes the LXX several times (e.g. Gen. i. 2 ;

---

[1] *Inconcussa...auctoritas divinae Scripturae, De Div. Nat.* 672 C. *Sacrae siquidem scripturae in omnibus sequenda est auctoritas, Ibid.* 509 A.

[2] See the critical notes in the Appendix.

[3] Guizot, *History of Civilization in France*, II. p. 372. Hegel, *Vorles. über Gesch. d. Phil.* pp. 160–1. Hjort, *Johannes Scotus Erigena, oder von dem Ursprung einer christlichen Philosophie*, p. 44.

[4] *De Div. Nat.* 555 A. Rufinus' version of Origen gives *invisibilis et incomposita* as the translation of the LXX text. *De Princ.* IV. 1. This is the reading in Augustine's Old Latin version also. *Conf.* XII. 21.

i. 21; iii. 7; Job xl. 14), and there are several cases where he varies from the Vulgate apparently under the influence of the LXX (e.g. Ps. xl. 6; Prov. viii. 22; Isa. xxvi. 10). It has been doubted whether he really did use the LXX, and it is true that in one of his earlier works he writes: *Septuaginta enim prae manibus non habemus*[1]. But this need not mean more than that he had not access to it then. It is perhaps possible that his quotations from it are borrowed from Jerome and other Fathers. He quotes the Greek Testament occasionally, but never for more than a single phrase (e.g. ἐν ἀρχῇ ἦν ὁ λόγος, John i. 1; εἰς μέτρον ἡλικίας, Eph. iv. 13; ἀνακεφαλαίωσις, Eph. i. 10).

The extant fragments of his Commentary on St John's Gospel, however, are sufficient to prove that he actually had the Greek text in his hands, for in correcting the Latin text, he remarks upon the tenses of the Greek verbs, and even comments upon a few various readings in the Greek manuscripts[2].

Many of the Fathers taught, like Origen, that there was a threefold, or, like Augustine, that there was a fourfold sense in the words of Scripture. But Erigena contends for an unlimited variety of significance. The multiplicity of truth in the Bible, he declares, in a beautiful image, is like the variety of colours in a peacock's feather, *siquidem in penna*

---

[1] *Expos. in Coel. Hier.* 243 A.

[2] Thus, for example, on John i. 15, he writes: *clamat vel sicut in Graeco legitur clamavit*, where the verb is κέκραγε; on John iii. 13, *ascendit ambiguum est, cujus temporis verbum sit, utrum praeteriti an praesentis. Sed in Graeco non est ambiguum; praeteriti temporis est*, where the verb is ἀναβέβηκεν; on John i. 18, *in sinu Patris, vel in sinibus Patris. In quibusdam codicibus Graecorum singulariter sinus Patris dicitur, in quibusdam pluraliter, quasi sinus multos Pater habeat*, where there was evidently a variant reading εἰς τοὺς κόλπους τοῦ Πατρός (like the Ἀβραὰμ καὶ Λάζαρον ἐν τοῖς κόλποις αὐτοῦ of Luke xvi. 24).

pavonis una eademque mirabilis ac pulchra innumerabilium colorum varietas conspicitur in uno eodemque loco ejusdem pennae portiunculae[1].

There is in Erigena's writings, as in those of all mediaeval authors, much allegorical interpretation of Scripture. It is carried to no worse lengths than in all his contemporaries; indeed, he is not nearly so fantastic as some mediaeval writers. Some good examples of this sort of exegesis are found in the exposition of the early pages of Genesis, which he gives in connection with his doctrine of creation. Thus the four rivers of Paradise are the four cardinal virtues— Pishon is prudence; Gihon, temperance; Hiddekel, fortitude; Euphrates, justice (816). The serpent is delight (*delectatio*); the woman, sense (*sensus*, αἴσθησις); the man, mind[2] (*mens*, νοῦς) (815). The fig-leaves represent the letter of the law, as against the spirit of it—mere leaves instead of nourishing fruit (839).

There is a good example of Erigena's allegorising method, as applied to the evangelical history, in the incident of the healing of the ten lepers, of whom only one returned to give thanks to our Lord. Leprosy, like sin, defaces the form of humanity, but does not altogether destroy it. Now human nature is tenfold. The body is fivefold, being compounded of the four elements with the addition of form. The soul (*anima*) is also fivefold, subsisting as intellect, reason, interior sense, exterior sense, and vital motion. When human nature is healed of the leprosy of sin, it will be no longer ten, but one, for it will be resolved into intellect alone, which will subsist for ever in pure contemplation of the truth. This is signified by the one leper who returned of the ten who were cleansed (874 A, B).

---

[1] *De Div. Nat.* 749 C.   [2] Augustine, *De Trin.* XII. 20.

Some of the Parables afford curious examples of this allegorical method of exposition. Thus, in the Parable of the Prodigal Son, the elder son represents the angels, the younger son humanity. The return of the wanderer is the return of the human race to God, through Christ, Who is typified by the slain calf. And, in the Parable of the Good Samaritan, the man who went down from Jerusalem to Jericho represents humanity, descending from Paradise into the world. The robbers are the Devil and his angels. The two points which this exposition of the Parable is intended to bring out are these—first, that there was little or no temporal interval, spent in Paradise, between the Creation and the Fall[1], for it is not written *A certain man was in Jerusalem*, but *A certain man went down from Jerusalem*; and second, that man fell in himself before the Devil tempted him[2], for he *went down from Jerusalem* before he *fell among robbers* (811).

There are several examples in which our philosopher lays uncritical stress upon the precise words of the Vulgate, and extracts a significance from them that they were never meant to possess. Thus, when we read that the earth produced plants and animals *in genere suo et secundum species suas*, we are to understand that the art of dialectic, which divides genera into species, and resolves species into genera, is not a human device, but is created in the nature of things, and by the Author of all arts that are true arts (748 D). And the Apostle's declaration that God calls the things that are

---

[1] Dante says that Adam was only seven hours in Paradise (*Paradiso*, XXXVI. 138–141). Thomas Aquinas somewhere makes the same statement.

[2] The thought is borrowed from Augustine. "The Devil, then, would not have ensnared man in the open and manifest sin of doing what God had forbidden, had man not already begun to live unto himself....The evil act had never been done had not an evil will preceded it." *De Civ. Dei*, XIV. 13.

not as though they were (*ea quae non sunt, tanquam ea quae sunt*) (Rom. iv. 17) is pressed into the service of Erigena's fundamental doctrine of being and non-being, by which all ultimate realities, because they surpass the reach of our intellect, are classed as *ea quae non sunt*—the superessential being equated, on the logical level, with the non-existent (445 C).

There is also a good deal of play upon words like *principium* and *verbum* in such passages as Gen. i. 1 and Ps. xlv. 1. *In principio creavit Deus coelum et terram* means that God created all in the Word (*in Verbo*) (556 B). And similarly *Eructavit cor meum verbum bonum, dico ego opera mea regi*, means that God makes all His works from the secret Word of His substance (*ex secreto substantiae meae Verbo*) (557 A).

These are characteristics which the Scot shares with all mediaeval expositors. He shares with commentators of all ages a tendency to emphasise a textual distinction when it serves his purpose. Thus he makes much of the difference between the two words in James i. 17, *Omne datum optimum et omne donum perfectum*, because he has a favourite doctrine of the contrast between the *datum* of nature and the *donum* of grace.

He occasionally avoids the plain meaning of Scripture by taking it interrogatively, or in some other sense that was never intended[1]. Thus in Gen. iii. 22: *And now, lest he put forth his hand, and take also of the Tree of Life, and eat, and live for ever, therefore the Lord God sent him forth from the Garden of Eden*, is taken to mean: *And now, may he not put forth his hand?* may he not reach forth in good deeds, and take of the spiritual gifts of God and eat the food of

---

[1] Erigena had Augustine as his exemplar in this method of treating Scripture. See *De Civ. Dei*, XVI. 6.

pure contemplation? (861-2). And in the Parable of the Ten Virgins, *Peradventure there will not be enough for us and you*, is taken in a similar way: *That haply there may be enough for us and you* (1017).

Our philosopher can achieve some astounding perversions of Scripture when it suits his purpose. When Paul said: *I knew not, brethren, that he was the High Priest*, it meant that the Apostle knew that he was *not* the High Priest, because Ananias was not High Priest by the ordinance of God, but through the superstition of the Jews! (595 C). And our Lord's declaration: *Of that day and of that hour knoweth no one, not even the angels in heaven, neither the Son* (which Erigena declares to be *obscurissimam questionem*), is interpreted to mean that He knew by prescience, but He did not know by experience, because the Judgment was not yet an accomplished fact (594-5). This particular perversion, however, Erigena borrowed from Epiphanius[1].

The sleep of Adam, and the severance of the sexes, though related as if they happened in Paradise, really came to pass after the first sin, and therefore out of Paradise. All this is related by anticipation (837). So with the opening of the tombs, and the resurrection of many of the saints at the death of Christ, for it is incredible that other tombs should open, before His own tomb opened, or that witnesses of the resurrection should rise, before He rose (837).

It is not good for man to be alone—an awkward text in view of Erigena's doctrine as to the separation of the sexes— is roundly said to be spoken in manifest irony (846 B). And,

---

[1] Erigena gives no reference, but it seems to be *De Fide*, XXI. and XXII., that he has in mind: ὁ δὲ πατὴρ οἶδε καὶ ἔπραξεν· ὁ δὲ Υἱὸς οἶδε μέν, οὐδέπω δὲ ἔπραξε· τουτέστιν· εἰ μὴ ὁ πατὴρ μόνος, οὔτε οἱ ἄγγελοι, οὔτε ὁ Υἱός. (57 B, C, Vol. 43, ed. Migne.)

elsewhere, when our philosopher has to admit that the sacred writers speak of a predestination to punishment and death, he simply declares that it is strained language (*abusivae locutionis*)[1].

It is natural to say, as most of those who have written on Erigena have said, that Erigena's greatest authorities among the Fathers are the pseudo-Dionysius and Maximus. He had translated both these authors, and had thus been brought into a very intimate contact with their thought. He quotes them frequently and largely, especially Dionysius—nearly one-seventh of the whole bulk of *The Divine Names* is quoted in *The Division of Nature*.

But while more than enough has been said in the past as to the influence of the pseudo-Dionysius and Maximus upon our philosopher, it is certain that Erigena's indebtedness to Augustine has never been sufficiently emphasised[2]. Augustine himself was so strongly influenced by Neoplatonism that there is naturally a considerable community of thought, on many points, between him and Dionysius, and it is often impossible to distinguish one source from another[3]. But Erigena constantly appeals to Augustine[4], and many of his

---

[1] *De Praed.* v. 3.

[2] It is necessary to stress this point as to the prime importance of Augustine as the source of Erigena's essential Neoplatonism. The ordinary view has made the pseudo-Dionysius practically the one and only source. We read, for example, that Erigena "was deeply influenced by the forms of Neo-Platonic thought transmitted through Dionysius, whose works he translated into Latin." (Thomas Whittaker, *The Neo-Platonists*, p. 188.) This, or some similar sentence, is regarded as a sufficient summary of the matter. The considerations enumerated above are enough to show that it is not. I have given detailed proof of the extent of Erigena's debt to Augustine in many notes.

[3] See L. Grandgeorge, *Saint Augustine et le Néo-platonisme* (1896), for Augustine's dependence on Plotinus and Porphyry, and his "profonde connaissance des doctrines néo-platoniciennes grâce aux traductions de Victorinus."

[4] There are twice as many quotations from Augustine as from Maximus in the *De Divisione Naturae*.

158   THE PHILOSOPHY OF ERIGENA

most characteristic thoughts and expressions are drawn
directly from the great African Father. It is impossible to
study Erigena's sources impartially without feeling that the
influence of Augustine counts for much more than has ever
been allowed in the past. The Scot's doctrine of evil, in
particular, he found in Augustine, and would have found
there if he had never heard of Dionysius[1]. It was in Augustine
that he found the pregnant sentence from which the whole
scheme of his philosophy is developed[2]. It is not too much
to say that some of Augustine's treatises, especially *The
City of God*, the *Confessions*[3], and *On the Trinity*, count for
more, in Erigena's essential thought, than the whole of the
Dionysian writings[4], with the *Ambigua* of Maximus thrown
into the scale.

Moreover, we have to remember (what is constantly
forgotten in this connection) that Erigena and all his contemporaries regarded Dionysius as of almost apostolic
authority and date. Was he not the convert of St Paul, and
the correspondent of St John and Timothy? Suppose that
Erigena found some particular doctrine in Augustine, before
he found it in Dionysius, and before he had even seen the
writings of Dionysius,—which must have happened again
and again, for the student bred in a cloister in Ireland was

[1] As Christlieb remarks there can be no doubt " dass sich Erigena für seine
Anschauung vom Bösen auf Augustin beruft und mit Recht berufen kann."
Leben u. Lehre d. Johannes Scotus Erigena, p. 385. See *De Civ. Dei*, XI. 9;
XIV. 11, 22, 23; *Conf.* VII. 12; *Enchir.* 11, 12, 13.
[2] *De Civ. Dei*, V. 9. There is probably some relation between the words of
Augustine and a passage in Aristotle, *Metaphysics*, XI. 7, where he distinguishes
between the unmoved and moving, the moved and moving, and the moved and
not moving.
[3] Particularly the eleventh and twelfth books.
[4] Staudenmaier agrees that Erigena depends upon Augustine more than upon
any of the Fathers. *Johannes Scotus Erigena u. d. Wissenschaft seiner Zeit*,
pp. 274–5.

sure to be familiar with Augustine from the beginning of his adult studies, and he had certainly not met with the writings of Dionysius until he found them in the Abbey of St Denys. He would, nevertheless, be likely to quote Dionysius for it because Dionysius carried such weight as an authority, and Erigena is always careful to support his theories, especially those which looked most novel and perilous, with the authority of Scripture and of the Fathers. As Kaftan has said, Dionysius "passed for a disciple of the Apostles, and seemed to a philosophy which attached itself to him to guarantee a direct connection with Christ and His Apostles[1]." In short, the fictitious importance of Dionysius as a revered authority in Erigena's own estimation is much greater than his real importance as an actual source of our philosopher's thoughts.

These considerations are confirmed by an examination of the relation between Erigena's principal work and his earlier treatise. In the tract *On Predestination* Dionysius is never cited, and none of the peculiarly Dionysian phrases are found. It is plain that the Scot had not met with the Areopagite until he was commissioned to translate his work into Latin. Only Latin Fathers are quoted,—Gregory the Great, and Isidore, each a single time, and Augustine, sixty times. But all the essential features of Erigena's thought are present. He is a Neoplatonist[2] in the tract *On Predestination* as

---

[1] Kaftan, *The Truth of the Christian Religion*, I. p. 158.

[2] "In reality he cannot be classed as a Neo-Platonist, for his whole effort was directed towards rationalising that system of dogmatic belief which the Neo-Platonists had opposed from the profoundest intellectual and ethical antipathy." (Thomas Whittaker, *The Neo-Platonists*, pp. 187–8.) This quaint dictum really amounts to saying that Erigena cannot be classed as a Neoplatonist because he was not a pagan. He is a Neoplatonist, then, let us say, as much as a Christian can be.

definitely as in *The Division of Nature*, though of course
the implications of the doctrine are not worked out as they
are in the larger treatise. The plain fact is *that Erigena got
all the Neoplatonist substance of his philosophy out of Augustine*,
and when he met with the pseudo-Dionysius he found (and
was doubtless delighted to find) the philosophic doctrine
which he had already made his own wrought out in more
detail, with more system, and with the supreme authority
of one who was an associate of the Apostles[1].

Of the Greek Fathers, besides the pseudo-Dionysius and
Maximus, Erigena quotes Origen[2], Gregory of Nyssa[3] and
Gregory Nazianzen[4], Basil[5], Epiphanius[6] and Chrysostom[7].

[1] "Les idées néoplatoniciennes qu'il émet à cette époque sont empruntées,
dans leurs principes au moins, aux ouvrages de saint-Augustin. Une seconde
période, déjà commencée en 858, est caracterisée par les traductions accomplies
par Jean Scot et la composition du *De Divisione Naturae*, son œuvre capitale.
Il a pris contact avec les auteurs grecs, et sa philosophie, qui s'en inspire,
devient tributaire du Pseudo-Denys." I quote this from an admirable article
on *Le néoplatonisme de Jean Scot*, by M. M. Jacquin, in the *Revue des Sciences
philosophiques et théologiques* (October 1907). The whole study confirms the
conclusion I had arrived at independently.

[2] *De Principiis*, III. (*De Div. Nat.* 929 A). *Ep. ad Romanos*, III. (*De Div.
Nat.* 922 C). Erigena used Rufinus' Latin version of Origen. I have established
this fact by a comparison of his quotations.

[3] *De Hominis Opificio* (*De Div. Nat. passim*). Erigena undoubtedly read
the Greek.

[4] Only through the medium of Maximus. I have carefully examined this
point, and proved that every passage that Erigena quotes is to be found in the
Ambigua.

[5] *Hexaemeron* (*De Div. Nat.* 521 A, 707 B, C, 709 B). Apparently Erigena
used a Latin version. Brilliantoff, the Russian scholar who has been investigating
the teaching of Erigena in its relation to the Greek Fathers, states positively,
however, that it was not that of Eustathius Afer (*Zeitschrift für wissenschaftliche
Theologie*, 47, 1904).

[6] *De Fide* (ἀγκυρωτός) (*De Div. Nat.* 601 C, etc.). Erigena certainly read
Epiphanius in Greek.

[7] *De Div. Nat.* 979 C, etc. Erigena seems to have used one of the numerous
Latin versions of Chrysostom.

He regards the two Gregories as one person—a confusion which he shared with his predecessor Alcuin[1].

[1] Erigena usually names Gregory of Nyssa, or Gregory the Theologian. Generally these references are correct, i.e. he usually refers the work *De Hominis Opificio* (which he calls *De Imagine*) to Gregory of Nyssa ; and where he names Gregory the Theologian the reference is nearly always to some writing of Gregory Nazianzen, in the exposition of Maximus. Thus in 877 C (*Gregorius Theologus in Epitaphio fratris sui Caesarii*) the reference is to *Orat.* VII., Εἰς Καισάριον τὸν ἑαυτοῦ ἀδελφὸν ἐπιτάφιος: in 835 A (*Gregorius Theologus in sermone de Paschate*) the reference is to *Orat.* XLV., Εἰς τὸ ἅγιον πάσχα: in 1005 B (*Maximus, exponens Gregorium Theologum in sermone de Nativitate*) the reference is to *Orat.* XXXVIII., Εἰς τὰ θεοφάνια: in 615 B (*Gregorius Theologus in primo sermone de Filio...Maximus exponit*) the reference is to *Orat.* XXIX., Περὶ Υἱοῦ.

There are one or two exceptions, however, to this general accuracy. Thus in 811 D–812 C (*Gregorius in decimo octavo capitulo sermonis de Imagine...Maximus, praefati Theologi expositor, sermonem ejus de Baptismo exponens*), where the first reference is to the *De Hominis Opificio* of Gregory of Nyssa, and the second to Gregory Nazianzen, *Orat.* XL., Εἰς τὸ ἅγιον βάπτισμα. And again in 879 C (*Gregorius Nyssaeus in sermone de Grandine*), where the reference is to Gregory Nazianzen, *Orat.* XVI., Εἰς τὸν πατέρα σιωπῶντα διὰ τὴν πληγὴν τῆς χαλάξης.

Erigena only names Gregory Nazianzen by that title three times. In two of these cases he expressly identifies him with Gregory of Nyssa. *Gregorius Nyssaeus, qui etiam Nazianzenus vocatur* (735 D), *Gregorius Nazianzenus, qui et Nyssaeus dicitur* (860 A). In the third passage he expressly distinguishes between them: *Ne videamur Nazianzeno Gregorio Theologo Nyssaeoque praedicto impudenter refragari, qui unanimiter certis approbant rationibus* (586 A).

It seems probable that the latter passage has been altered by a scribe, for one of the manuscripts omits *Nyssaeoque praedicto* and reads *approbat* for *approbant*. This particular manuscript certainly presents us with the original text in some other instances: for example, in a later passage (899 C) it reads *Ancoratum*, which is correct (in a reference to the ἀγκυρωτός of Epiphanius), where other manuscripts read *accuratum*.

There is no doubt at all, I think, that Erigena believed the two Gregories to be one person. The general accuracy of his references seems to be due to the fact that when he was quoting Gregory Nazianzen, he referred to him in the way that he found him described in Maximus, as Gregory the Theologian; while he evidently had access to a copy of *De Hominis Opificio*, which bore the name of the author, Gregory of Nyssa. He had met with references to Gregory Nazianzen also, and he took *Gregorius Nazianzenus*, *Gregorius Nyssaeus* and *Gregorius Theologus* to be different designations of the same person.

It is significant that Erigena's great predecessor Alcuin also confused the two

Next to Augustine, Erigena unquestionably owes most to Gregory of Nyssa, and the whole of his indebtedness is to the one work entitled, *On the Creation of Man*, περὶ κατασκευῆς ἀνθρώπου, which he consistently quotes as *De Imagine*[1].

Gregories. *Beatus quoque Gregorius Nazianzenus vel Nyssaeus episcopus erudi-tissimus* (*De Processione Spiritus Sancti*, c. 66 D, Vol. 101, ed. Migne).

The question as to Erigena's confusion of the two Gregories has been touched upon, not very conclusively, by Dr Johannes Draeseke, in his monograph *Johannes Scotus Erigena und dessen Gewährsmänner* (Leipzig, 1902), and in his article *Zu Scotus Erigena Bemerkungen und Mittheilungen* (in *Zeitschrift für wissenschaftliche Theologie*, 47 (1904)).

[1] Erigena certainly read the *De Hominis Opificio* of Gregory of Nyssa in Greek. The language of his quotations proves this. M. Felix Ravaisson, in discussing the authorship of an unpublished manuscript which he believes to be by Erigena, remarked, as evidence, the frequent citation "de mots grecs et quelquefois des mots grecs latinisés....Or, on sait que Scot Érigène aimât à faire ainsi étalage de ses connaissances dans la langue grecque" (Floss, p. 9). This is too unqualified a statement. It is true that Erigena sprinkles his pages with Greek words, but generally these are more or less technical terms, such as οὐσία, ὑπόστασις, καταφατική, ἀποφατική, ἀνάλυσις, ἄναρχος, and the like. It is only, I think, when he is *actually citing an author whom he read in Greek* that it is otherwise—then we find him casually quoting some Greek words as they stand, and latinising others. I had formed a strong impression, on general grounds, that Erigena read Gregory of Nyssa's *De Hominis Opificio*, and Epiphanius' *De Fide*, in Greek, and that he read the other Greek Fathers with whom he was acquainted, Origen, Chrysostom, and Basil, in Latin versions. On going into detail I found the principle stated above verified in his citations. In his quotations from Gregory of Nyssa there are many examples of Greek words, in their original form, or latinised, *in situ*.

Compare the following examples—the first reference in each case is to Erigena's *De Divisione Naturae*, and the second to Gregory of Nyssa's *De Hominis Opificio* (in the edition of Migne, Vol. 44)—*...quae circa subjectum theorizantur...*, 502 C; *...τινὶ τῶν περὶ τὸ ὑποκείμενον θεωρουμένον*, 213 A. *Dicunt enim, hominem μικρόκοσμον, id est, parvum mundum esse*, 793 C; *φασὶ γὰρ μικρὸν εἶναι κόσμον τὸν ἄνθρωπον*, 177 D. *Deinde epanalepsin, id est, repetitionem facit secundum constitutionem sermonis...*, 795 A; *εἶτα ἐπανάληψιν ποιεῖται τοῦ κατὰ τὴν κατασκευὴν λόγου...*, 181 A. *Lignum illud...cui nomen est πᾶν, id est, omne...*, 819 C; *τὸ ξύλον ἐκεῖνο...ᾧ ὄνομά ἐστι τὸ πᾶν...*, 196 D.

His quotations from Epiphanius are fewer and shorter, but there are a few examples of the same sort. Compare the following—the first reference in each

It is true that he quotes largely from Maximus, but the quotations are nearly all expositions of ideas that are to be found also in Dionysius and in Gregory of Nyssa. Gregory Nazianzen, though Maximus was his professed expositor, counts for very much less, as a source of ideas, than his namesake of Nyssa. There is little in Gregory the Theologian that Erigena did not find elsewhere, and little in Maximus (with one important exception) but the detailed exposition of what he found elsewhere.

In short, Erigena's dependence upon the Fathers is mainly upon Gregory of Nyssa in the East, and upon Augustine in the West.

Of the Latin Fathers, besides Augustine, he quotes Ambrose[1] and Jerome[2] occasionally, and Hilary[3], Gregory the Great[4], and Isidore[5], each a single time.

case is again to the *De Divisione Naturae*, the second to Epiphanius' *De Fide* (in the edition of Migne, Vol. 43): κάνθαροι, *hoc est, scabrones, futuram sui mortem sentientes...*, 900 B; κάνθαροι δὲ μέλλοντες τελευτᾶν, 173 B. *Sicut ipsa revelant*, φῶς, πῦρ, πνεῦμα, *hoc est, lux, ignis, spiritus*, 742 C; καθὼς ἑαυτὰ ἀποκαλύπτει, φῶς, πῦρ, πνεῦμα, 140 A.

In respect to the pseudo-Dionysius and Maximus the case is somewhat different, for Erigena had previously issued formal Latin translations of these authors, and therefore he was not reading off an impromptu version of a passage in order to quote it. But in these translations themselves there are examples of a similar kind to those given above (though fewer in proportion, I think), e.g. ὄν, ἀορασίαν, *sophia, elicoeides, anagogen*.

In his quotations from Origen, Basil, and Chrysostom (except that he once cites the Greek title of Origen's great work, περὶ ἀρχῶν) there are never, I believe, any Greek words quoted as they stand in the text, or latinised. And, in the case of Origen, I have proved, by comparing the quotations, that Erigena used the version of Rufinus.

[1] *Hexaemeron* (*De Div. Nat.* 705 C, etc.), *De Paradiso* (*De Div. Nat.* 830 D, etc.), *Expos. in Lucam* (*De Div. Nat.* 878 B, etc.).

[2] *Expos. Ezechiel* (*De Div. Nat.* 960 C, 1004 A). (See also 269 A.)

[3] *De Trinitate*, III. 16 (*De Div. Nat.* 992 B).

[4] *Moral. in Job*, XI. 5 (*De Praed.* 425 B).

[5] *Sentent.* II. 6 (*De Praed.* 366 D).

Erigena borrowed the method of the *theologia affirmativa et abnegativa*, and his doctrine of the primal causes, from Dionysius. The latter conception is the one point on which he is peculiarly indebted to the Areopagite, as against much else that was to be found in the Dionysian writings, but was also to be found elsewhere in the writers that the Scot knew. His doctrine of the Trinity is wholly from Augustine. His doctrine of evil he found fully developed both in Augustine and in Dionysius, and he was certainly familiar with Augustine first. His thought as to time and space and formless matter is also from Augustine. Apart from the last point his theory of matter is almost exclusively from Gregory of Nyssa, and his teaching as to the image of God in man is mainly from the same source. So is his doctrine of the resurrection, though it also owes something to Gregory Nazianzen and to Epiphanius. His theory of the restoration of all things is almost entirely from Origen. From Maximus he got a few favourite metaphors, and a single thought that is important, because it modified, in a profoundly Christian sense, the Neoplatonist doctrine of the pseudo-Dionysius— the thought that all the divisions of the world are united in Christ, and through Him in redeemed humanity[1].

Erigena's references to Basil, Chrysostom, Ambrose, Jerome, and Hilary, are almost all on exegetical points.

No philosopher was ever less original, in the narrower sense, than Erigena. It would be easy to find in the pseudo-Dionysius, Maximus, Origen, Gregory of Nyssa, and Augus-

---

[1] In der Hauptidee, um welche sich das System des Erigena bewegt, dass in dem Menschen, als der vermittelnden Einheit, durch die Vermittlung Christi alle Differenzen aufgehoben, der Unterschied und die Einheit in ihm auf gleiche Weise gesetzt sind, folgte Erigena in Allgemeinen ganz dem Maximus. Baur, *Lehre v. d. Dreieinigkeit*, II. p. 270.

tine, a source for almost every single thought in the Scot's system[1]. Yet, on the other hand, he is by no means a mere compiler, for he has wrought all these thoughts into an impressive scheme, and he has done it with remarkable skill and subtlety[2]. The form and the system are his, and that is no small praise. It was only a metaphysician of great insight who could have found all that he needed in the incomplete and disorderly literature to which he had access, and it was only a philosopher of great speculative power who could have wrought it all into so massive a system[3].

[1] Berücksichtigt man nun die ganze Lehre des Erigena, so muss man allerdings zugestehen, dass wenige Gedanken darin sich vorfinden, die nicht sehen eines älteren Ursprunges wären; namentlich sind es die Grundideen des Neuplatonismus, welche mit manchen Reminiscenzen an Aristoteles die Grundlage bilden, womit sich bei ihm einzelne Lehren der Kirche und der Kirchenväter zu einem Ganzen verbunden haben. Kaulich, *Entwicklung der scholastischen Philosophie von Johannes Scotus Erigena bis Abälard*, p. 222.

[2] Hauréau, answering the criticism that Erigena is "un interprète plus fidèle qu'inventif," says, with great justice: "Souvent, à la vérité, il cite Platon, et il le commente souvent à la manière des Alexandrins, qu'il ne cite pas; mais nous ne croyons pas devoir, à cause de cela, lui refuser le génie de l'inventeur. A notre avis, ce philosophe érudit a reçu de l'antiquité le fond même de sa doctrine; mais il a reproduit cette doctrine sous une forme nouvelle." *Histoire de la philosophie scolastique*, I. p. 161.

Huber, the ablest of all Erigena's commentators, remarks: "Wenn an Erigena zuletzt sich wenig originales entdecken lässt und wir für die meisten seiner Ideen Vorgänger aufzufinden im Stande sind, wenn er in dieser gelehrigen und mehr receptiven als productiven Haltung wieder ganz als ein Kind des Mittelalters sich zeigt, das erst seine Erziehung und Bildung von fremder Autorität zu gewinnen hatte—diese Vereinigung, die sich in ihm durch sein philosophisches, die Einheit einer Weltanschauung forderndes Genie und durch sein Studium der Patristik unbewusst vermittelte, ist seine eigenste That." *Johannes Scotus Erigena*, p. 431.

[3] Malgré ces inconséquences, le système de Scot Erigène est une œuvre incomparable de profondeur spéculative, si l'on songe à l'état intellectuel de l'époque qui l'a vu naître. A. Jundt, *Histoire de panthéisme populaire au moyen âge*, p. 12. An Trieb und Kraft zu systematischer Bildung ist er ein Phänomen, und mit Recht verehren ihn die speculativen Philosophen als einen Meister. Harnack, *Dogmengeschichte*, III. p. 270.

The general affinity of Erigena's thought, and indeed the main outline of it, may be traced back through Dionysius, Maximus, Gregory of Nyssa, and Augustine, to Proclus, Plotinus, and thence, in its germ, to Plato. But it is certain that Erigena knew nothing of Plato except the *Timaeus*, and that only in the Latin translation of Chalcidius[1]. He calls Plato "the greatest philosopher in the world[2]," but he never quotes anything except the *Timaeus*, and fond as he is of interlarding Greek with his Latin, he never quotes a single Greek word from it.

It is unfortunate that Erigena knew so little of Plato, and perhaps unfortunate that what he did know was the *Timaeus*. For that dialogue contains little but Plato's elaborate cosmology, and thus it is only at an unimportant point in Erigena's system, and one that has inevitably gone out of date, that the Scot draws directly from the greatest of the Greek philosophers. He refers to the *Timaeus* four times.

His first reference is to Plato's famous conception of the universe as an animal[3]—*hunc mundum visibilem, quasi magnum quoddam animal, corpore animaque componi; cujus animalis corpus quidem est quattuor elementis notissimis generalibusque, diversisque corporibus ex eisdem compositis compactum; anima vero ipsius est generalis vita, quae omnia,*

[1] Hauréau says: "Il a lu sans doute le texte original du *Timée* de Platon, dont il doit exister des exemplaires dans les bibliothèques monastiques de l'Irlande" (*Histoire de la philosophie scolastique*, I. p. 152). But the reason given above is absolutely conclusive against this opinion, for anyone who has taken note of Erigena's habit of quotation. Duhem agrees with the statement in the text that Erigena knew the *Timaeus* only "par l'intermédiaire de la traduction et du commentaire dont Chalcidius est l'auteur" (*Le Système du Monde*, III. p. 46).

[2] *Plato, philosophantium de mundo maximus. De Div. Nat.* 476 C. *Plato, philosophorum summus. Ibid.* 728 A.

[3] δεῖ λέγειν τόνδε τὸν κόσμον ζῷον ἔμψυχον ἔννουν τε τῇ ἀληθείᾳ διὰ τὴν τοῦ Θεοῦ γενέσθαι πρόνοιαν. *Timaeus*, 30.

quae in motu atque in statu sunt vegetat atque movet[1]. This does not correspond verbally with any passage in the *Timaeus*, but it is a fair summary of Plato's teaching in the dialogue upon this point. It is practically a combination of the several passages that contain the conception[2].

There is another passage where Erigena does not mention the *Timaeus* but refers to the opinion of Plato, *philosophorum summus, et qui circa eum sunt*[3], as to the general life of the world. But the Scot never really develops the notion of the universe as a living organism—never elaborates it as Giordano Bruno did, for example.

Erigena's next reference to the *Timaeus* is in relation to his doctrine of formless matter. He says that Plato states that formless matter is capacity of form; *informem materiam esse formarum capacitatem*[4]. This, again, is a condensation of Plato's obscure theory. In the *Timaeus* he teaches that there exists an indeterminate something which is the source of becoming (ἐκεῖνο ἐν ᾧ γίγνεται), a sort of receptacle of generation (πάσης γενέσεως ὑποδοχή), a matrix which underlies all things (ἐκμαγεῖον γὰρ φύσει παντὶ κεῖται), a formless principle out of which all things are formed[5]. Erigena's theory of formless matter, however, might have been found in Augustine[6], if he had never heard of Plato, and probably was found there, before he had read the *Timaeus*.

The other references to the *Timaeus* are quite casual, and

---

[1] *De Div. Nat.* 476 C.
[2] *Timaeus*, 10, 11, 13, 30, 44, 73.
[3] *De Div. Nat.* 728 A.
[4] *De Div. Nat.* 500 C.
[5] *Timaeus*, 24.
[6] *Conf.* XII. *passim.*

merely relate to what Plato says about the planets[1], and about the life of plants[2].

There are a few other points, where Erigena makes no mention of the *Timaeus*, but where the influence of the dialogue may perhaps be traced. There is the general conception of goodness as essentially creative. And there is the thought of time as generated with the universe. But the first thought Erigena might have found, more fully worked out, in Dionysius[3], and the second in Augustine[4], if he had never seen Plato at all. And there is also Plato's suggestion that there could be nothing visible without fire, and nothing tangible without earth, which Erigena develops into a theory of the five senses, arguing that the senses represent the four elements which compose the body, since there is no sight where there is not fire, no touch where there is not earth, no hearing where there is not air, and neither smell nor taste where there is not water[5]. This is perhaps the one instance in which Erigena directly borrowed and developed a thought of Plato's.

There is very little in the *Timaeus* about Plato's characteristic doctrine of ideas—the very point at which we might have expected Erigena's contact with Plato to be most fruitful. There is indeed some mention of the self-existing patterns, invisible, imperceptible by the senses, and only to be apprehended by pure intellect[6], but the conception of

---

[1] *Timaeus*, 14 (*De Div. Nat.* 698 A).

[2] *Ibid.* 55 (*De Div. Nat.* 735 C).

[3] *De Div. Nom.* IV. 3, 10, 23; V. 6. Also in Origen, *De Princ.* II. 9. 6.

[4] *Conf.* XI. *passim*.

[5] *De Div. Nat.* 733 B. I do not know whether it has been pointed out before, but the notion in Plato seems to be derived from a saying of Empedocles. The fragment is quoted in Burnet, *Early Greek Philosophy*, p. 255 (1908).

[6] *Timaeus*, 25, 26.

their activity is not worked out as it is elsewhere in Plato. And all Erigena's doctrine of the creative ideas seems to have come bodily from Dionysius. There is, of course, no doubt at all that Erigena's doctrine of the primal causes derives ultimately from the Platonic doctrine of ideas, but Plato's thought had been developed through Proclus and Dionysius, and it is from a passage in the Areopagite[1] that Erigena expressly begins his own development of the notion of the *causae primordiales*.

We may be equally certain that Erigena did not know Proclus, Plotinus or Philo at first hand. He never quotes any of them, and, judging from his habits with the authors that he knew, he would certainly have cited them copiously if he had had access to them.

We arrive, therefore, at the rather paradoxical position that Erigena, who became the principal medium by which the thoughts of Neoplatonism passed over into the mysticism of the later Middle Ages, and into some of the Renaissance philosophies[2], had never himself come into direct contact with any of the great Neoplatonist writers, and had only a very slight and secondhand knowledge of Plato himself.

Erigena refers to Aristotle as *acutissimus apud Graecos naturalium rerum discretionis repertor*[3], and in another place[4] claims him *cum suis sectatoribus* as approving the opinion

---

[1] *De Div. Nom.* v. 8 (*ad fin.*).

[2] Daher ist uns der Pseudodionys der erste, Maximus der zweite, Erigena der dritte und hauptsächlichste Pfeiler der Brücke, auf welcher der Platonismus je mit besonderen Modificationen in die abendländische Speculation überging, ohne dass natürlich damit die Bedeutung vieler griechischer Väter, besonders des Origenes und der Alexandriner überhaupt, für die Fortpflanzung der griechischen Philosophie geläugnet sein soll. Christlieb, *Leben u. Lehre d. Johannes Scotus Erigena*, p. 90.

[3] *De Div. Nat.* 462 D.

[4] *Ibid.* 870 A.

that grammar and rhetoric are not, like dialectic, grounded in the nature of things, but only in the usage of language, *non secundum naturam, sed secundum consuetudinem loquentium.* But it is certain that he had none of Aristotle's writings, except the *Categoriae* and the *De Interpretatione* in the Latin translation of Boethius[1].

He betrays no knowledge of the Greek classics, though he refers (without mentioning Homer or the *Odyssey*) to the incident of the recognition of Ulysses by his dog[2]. Among classical Latin authors he quotes Virgil[3], Cicero[4], and the elder Pliny[5], and of later writers, Boethius[6]—*magnificus Boethius*, as he more than once calls him—and Martianus Capella[7], the African Neoplatonist of the fifth century.

[1] *De Div. Nat.* 478 C, 597 C, 870 A.

[2] *Ibid.* 738.

[3] *Aeneid*, VI. 724–6 (*De Div. Nat.* 476 D) and XII. 906 (*De Div. Nat.* 550 B); *Georg.* II. 325–6 (*De Div. Nat.* 712 C).

[4] *De Div. Nat.* 461 B. *De Praed.* XV. 7. But probably Erigena only knew the *Topica* in the commentary of Boethius.

[5] *De Div. Nat.* 719 A, 721 C, 735 C. These are statements from the *Historia Naturalis*, whence also Erigena evidently got his references to Pythagoras and Eratosthenes. All these references are in the section which Erigena devotes to the physical science of his day. Erigena's mention of Plinius Secundus (Plinius secundus, as Floss prints it) has misled Huber into a reference to "der jünger Plinius." It has led Noack, in his German translation of the *De Divisione Naturae*, into a similar error, for he twice renders: "Plinius der Zweite" (I. p. 386 and p. 389. *De Div. Nat.* 719 A and 721 C).

[6] *De Arithmetica* (*De Div. Nat.* 498 B, 655 A). *De Trinitate* (*De Div. Nat.* 877 B).

[7] *De Div. Nat.* 719 A, 720 B. The references are to the *De Nuptiis Philologiae et Mercurii.* The book consists of sections dealing with the seven liberal arts—Grammar, Dialectic, Rhetoric, Geometry, Arithmetic, Astronomy, and Music—linked together by a rather inane allegory of the marriage of Mercury and Philologia, to whom seven bondwomen (the arts) are given as a wedding portion. It became a sort of encyclopaedia for the Middle Ages.

V. THE INFLUENCE OF ERIGENA UPON LATER TIMES

IT is very difficult to estimate the real extent of the influence of Erigena upon succeeding generations. It has often been supposed that such an influence hardly existed at all, and that the Scot's speculations were buried with him. It may be admitted at once that the character of his thought was alien to the general mind of his own age. The Papal ban upon his writings, too, would make against any widespread influence of an acknowledged kind in the later Middle Ages. Yet these facts would not make it less likely for his doctrine to influence such mediaeval thinkers as were more subtle and more adventurous than the rest. It follows, from similar considerations, that if the teaching of Erigena had any popular influence in the Middle Ages, we should expect to find it among the heretical sects which abounded in the twelfth and thirteenth centuries.

The instances in which we have definite knowledge of the intellectual influence of Erigena upon mediaeval times confirm these expectations. The known points of contact and the larger connections which they suggest may be briefly summarised.

It appears from the fourth canon of the Synod of Langres, that the Scot had many disciples and admirers in his own lifetime[1]. We know that he considerably influenced Heric of Auxerre, and his pupil, Remigius[2], and also Gerbert,

---

[1] Huber, *Johannes Scotus Erigena*, p. 50.
[2] R. L. Poole, *Illustrations of the History of Medieval Thought*, p. 75. Traube considers, in this connection, "dass man von einer unmittelbaren Schule und Nachfolge des irischen Meisters sprechen darf" (*Quellen u. Untersuchungen z. Lat. Phil. des Mittelalters*, I. 2. 1906).

afterward Pope Silvester the Second[1]. Then it is beyond
doubt that Berengar of Tours had read Erigena. The Scot
was much mentioned in the Berengarian controversy about
the Eucharist, and he was associated with Berengar in the
condemnation of his sacramental doctrine by the Councils
of Vercelli, in 1050, and of Rome, in 1059. In the *Sententiae*
of Anselm of Laon there is a passage on the allegorical
interpretation of the fruits of Paradise in which the *Doctor
scholasticus* refers to the *liber qui intitulatur perifision quem
Crisostomus dicitur fecisse*[2]. It is certain that the speculations
of that remarkable man, Gilbert de la Porrée[3], were much
indebted to Erigena[4]. Gilbert wrote an extensive commentary on the *Tractates on the Trinity*, ascribed to Boethius[5],

[1] M. de Wulf, *Histoire de la philosophie médiévale*, p. 198.

[2] The passage is f. 90 D. It is pointed out in Dr Bliemetzrieder's *Anselms
von Laon Systematische Sentenzen*, p. 22, that the epithet *Chrysostomis* is also
given to the Scot by Honorius of Autun, *De Scriptoribus Ecclesiasticis*, III.
12. He might have added that Honorius also uses the phrase of Erigena in the
introduction to the *Clavis Physicae*.

Le *De divisione naturae* qui domine de si haut toutes les œuvres philosophiques de son siècle et des deux siècles suivants se voit condamné par l'Eglise et
rejeté par les philosophes. Mais en même temps qu'on le condamne, on voit en
lui le modèle de l'œuvre à reprendre et à refaire. Les premières sommes théologiques ou sentences systématiques, celle d'Anselme de Laon par exemple, lui
doivent la largeur de vues et le sens de l'ordre qui les élèvent au-dessus des
compilations sans nombre de leur temps. E. Gilson, *La Philosophie au Moyen
Age*, I. p. 26.

[3] Notwithstanding Matthew Arnold's gibe at him for his opposition to
Bernard, "Now not one in ten Recalls the obscure opposer he outweighed"—
Gilbert was a thinker, and intellectually an abler man than the great Abbot of
Clairvaux.

[4] Duhem, *Le Système du Monde*, v. p. 238. Kaulich, *Entwicklung der
scholastischen Philosophie von Johannes Scotus Erigena bis Abälard*, p. 24.
R. L. Poole, *Illustrations of the History of Medieval Thought*, p. 180.

[5] The ascription of the *Tractates on the Trinity* to Boethius has been
generally regarded as false by modern scholars, until quite recently. The
discovery of a fragment of Cassiodorus, in which he ascribes to Boethius "a

and the whole work manifests Erigena's influence. Forty years after the trial of Gilbert de la Porrée the number of his disciples was so large as to alarm Geoffrey, the Abbot of Clairvaux[1], who had inherited Bernard's bias against Gilbert's teaching. A still more famous antagonist of Bernard's, no less a man than Abailard himself, also appears to have been influenced by the Scot[2]. So undoubtedly was Honorius of Autun in a very large degree. He quotes Erigena's phrases and imitates his style, and the *Clavis Physicae, de Naturis Rerum* is, as the preface states, a compilation, *excerptis ab Honorio solitario de quinque libris cuiusdam Chrisostomi,* viz. *The Division of Nature.* Wibald, the Abbot of Corvey, writing in 1149, refers to Erigena as the last of a line of great teachers beginning with Bede[3]. Simon of Tournai frequently cites Erigena in his *Summa theologica,* and, indeed, follows the Scot as his master[4]. Richard of St Victor also mentions him as one of the great pioneers of theology[5], while we know that the Victorine school of mystics was generally influenced by Erigena's writings and translations to a very considerable extent[6].

book on the Trinity, some dogmatic chapters, and a book against Nestorius," along with the criticism of some German and American scholars, has definitely re-established the mediaeval view. See the Introduction by Dr H. F. Stewart and Dr E. K. Rand to their edition of *The Theological Tractates and the Consolation of Philosophy* (1918), and Draeseke, *Johannes Scotus Erigena und seine Gewährsmänner,* pp. 15–16 (Leipzig, 1902).

[1] R. L. Poole, *Illustrations of the History of Medieval Thought,* p. 199.

[2] M. de Wulf, *Histoire de la philosophie médiévale,* p. 198.

[3] *Quid loquar de caeteris viris doctissimis qui post predictos in ecclesia Dei scribendo et disserendo preclara ingenii sui monimenta reliquerunt? Bedam, dico, et Ambrosium Aupertum, Heimonem, Rabanum, Johannem Scottum, et multos preterea, quorum opera legimus. Epist.* 167. Quoted in Poole, p. 78.

[4] Hauréau, *Notices et Extraits,* III. p. 253.

[5] *Exceptionum,* I. 24.

[6] Erdmann, *History of Philosophy,* I. p. 333.

About the end of the twelfth century *The Division of Nature* was found in the hands of a heretical sect in France, and Gauthier le Cornu, Archbishop of Sens, denounced it as full of abominable blasphemies[1]. We have evidence that new manuscripts of Erigena's great work were being copied in Germany in the same century[2]. It is stated that the book was also found in wide circulation among the Albigenses in the south of France, and that the action of Pope Honorius the Third in 1225 was partly at least in consequence of this fact[3]. It is almost certain (though the whole region of those weltering heresies is extremely obscure) that Erigena's work was also influential among many other heretical sects of the Middle Ages,—the Catharists, the Beghards, the Brothers and Sisters of the Free Spirit, and so forth[4].

It has been pointed out that there are not many traces of Erigena in the later Middle Ages, and that the great Schoolmen, Anselm, Albert the Great, Thomas Aquinas, Bonaventura, and Duns Scotus, never mention him[5]. After the Papal condemnation that is not surprising[6], but it should

---

[1] Hauréau, *Histoire de la philosophie scolastique*, I. p. 175.

[2] Dr J. Draeseke, in *Zeitschrift für wissenschaftliche Theologie*, 47 (1904).

[3] Staudenmaier, *Johannes Scotus Erigena und die Wissenschaft seiner Zeit*, p. 205. Schlüter (in Floss, 103). Manitius, *Geschichte d. lat. Literatur d. Mittelalters*, p. 329.

[4] There is some evidence connecting these sects with Amalric of Bena and David of Dinant and generally with the teaching of Erigena. See Mosheim, *Ecclesiastical History*, Pt. II. 5. 12. Gieseler, *Ecclesiastical History*, III. p. 467. Christlieb, *Leben u. Lehre d. Johannes Scotus Erigena*, p. 440. In fact, it has been roundly said that "on trouve l'influence de Scot dans toutes les déformations populaires de la mystique." M. de Wulf, *Histoire de la philosophie médiévale*, p. 199.

[5] Huber, *Johannes Scotus Erigena*, p. 432.

[6] There is much to confirm the suspicion that Erigena's great work was often read and used when it was not explicitly quoted. "Ja es hat den Ausschein, dass die Schriften des Erigena geradezu als Quelle benützt wurden, obwohl sein

be remembered that there are unquestionable lines of communication. It is almost certain that Avicebron depended, to some considerable extent, on Erigena[1], and it is unnecessary to enlarge upon the influence which he exerted upon the Schoolmen. In fact it has been roundly said that in accepting the philosophy of Avicebron they were really recovering their own tradition, and returning to the earlier Latin scholastic which was represented by Erigena[2]. Moreover, the influence of Erigena reached some of the Schoolmen, and notably Thomas Aquinas, by way of the commentary of Gilbert de la Porrée on Boethius' *Tractates on the Trinity*[3]. It should also be remembered that Thomas Aquinas and Albert the Great deal in some detail with the heresy of Amalric of Bena and David of Dinant, which was a revival of Erigena's doctrine.

Amalric of Bena taught in the University of Paris in the early years of the thirteenth century. After gaining repute by his lectures on dialectics, he began to lecture on theology, and created a sensation by his doctrines. The University

---

Name nicht genannt wird." W. Kaulich, *Entwicklung der scholastischen Philosophie von Johannes Scotus Erigena bis Abälard*, p. 23. As an example, a passage about dialectic (*De Div. Nat.* 749 A) is quoted in a treatise on sacramental doctrine, entitled *De corpore et sanguine Domini*, formerly ascribed to Gerbert, and now believed to be the work of Heriger of Lobbes, but Erigena's name is not mentioned.

[1] Duhem, *Le Système du Monde*, v. pp. 38-75.

[2] En accueillant la philosophie d'Ibn Gabirol, la Scolastique latine ne faisait que reprendre son bien. *Ibid.* v. p. 236.

[3] Sans doute, avec le traité de Boëce, Saint Thomas a en mains le commentaire de Gilbert de la Porrée, dont l'influence transparaît en divers passages de son opuscule (*De Ente et Essentia*). Cette influence rattache encore la pensée du Docteur dominicain à la tradition de l'ancienne Scolastique latine, et cela d'une manière d'autant plus complète que les réflexions de Gilbert de la Porrée au sujet de l'οὐσία gardent comme un souvenir des doctrines de Jean Scot Érigène. *Ibid.* v. p. 473.

condemned his teaching, and expelled him, in 1204. He appealed to the Pope, Innocent the Third, who confirmed the decision. In 1207 he returned to Paris, and recanted. He died soon afterward. Some of his disciples were burned at Champeaux in 1210, and others at Amiens, in the following year.

The principal source of our knowledge of Amalric's doctrine is a statement by Cardinal Henry of Ostia. He derived his facts from Odo Tusculanus, who was the episcopal chancellor at Paris, and had evidently drawn up a formal list of Amalric's errors. The Cardinal describes the work of John the Scot, which is named *Periphysion, id est, De Natura*, as the source of Amalric's heresies, and he mentions the Scot's dependence upon Maximus. Among the many heresies of the book he defines three—first and greatest, that all is God (quoting the very words of Erigena, that "it is not easy to deny that the creature and the Creator are one")[1]; second, that the primordial causes, which are called ideas, both create and are created; third, that in the consummation of all things there will be a reunion of the sexes which is already begun in Christ[2].

---

[1] *De Div. Nat.* 528 B.

[2] *Impii Almarici dogma istud colligitur in libro magistri Johannis Scoti qui dicitur Periphysion, id est, De Natura. Quem secutus est iste Almaricus, de quo hic loquitur, sed et dictus Johannes in eodem libro auctoritates cujusdam magistri graeci nomine Maximi introduxit. In quo libro qui et per magistros damnatus fuit Parisiis, multae haereses continentur. De quibus gratia exempli sufficiat tangere tres errores. Primus et summus error est quod omnia sunt Deus; unde dicit: Motum Deo dare non possum. Et sequitur; cum in ipso sint omnia et cum ipse sit omnia. Et alibi in eodem libro dicitur, non facile posse negari creaturam et creatorem idem esse.........Secundus est, quod primordiales causae, quae vocantur ideae, id est, forma seu exemplar, creant et creantur: cum tamen secundum sanctos idem sint quod Deus: in quantum sunt in Deo; et ideo creari non possunt. De quibus tamen et idem liber loqui intendit.*

Martin of Troppau, otherwise called Martin of Poland, who died in 1278, wrote a *Chronicle*[1] of the Popes—he had been Chaplain to Clement the Fourth, Gregory the Tenth, Innocent the Fifth, John the Twenty-first, and Nicholas the Third—and in his account of the Fourth Lateran Council he gives another statement of the errors of Amalric. He tells us that Amalric taught that the ideas which exist in the mind of God both create and are created; that God is called the end of all things, since all things return to Him and rest immutably in Him; that as the light cannot be perceived in itself, but only as diffused through the air, so God cannot be seen, as He is, either by men or by angels, but He can be contemplated in His creatures; that the distinction of the sexes is due to sin, for if man had not sinned, he would have multiplied like the angels; and that after the resurrection the sexes will be reunited, as they were at the creation. All these errors, writes the chronicler (in lamentable Latin) are found in the book, *qui intytulatur Periphysion, qui ponitur inter alios libros perysios (Parisiis) dampnatos, et dicitur liber Amalrici qui Amalricus combustus fuit perysius (Parisiis) cum sequacibus suis*[2].

Everything goes to show that Amalric's doctrine was a genuine revival of Erigena's system, without any particular perversion or development. Among his followers, however, the teaching seems to have had a pietistic rather than a

---

Tertius est quod per consummationem seculi erit adunatio sexuum, sive non erit distinctio sexus, quam adunationem in Christo asserit incepisse.... See Huber, *Johannes Scotus Erigena*, pp. 435–6; Gieseler, *Ecclesiastical History*, III. p. 299.

[1] *Martini Poloni Chronica Summorum Pontificum Imperatorumque*, Basle, 1559.

[2] Huber, *Johannes Scotus Erigena*, p. 437. Gieseler, *Ecclesiastical History*, III. p. 300.

philosophical character—the Amalricians, in fact, were mystics.

Some of them taught a doctrine of the three dispensations, which somewhat resembles that of Joachim of Flora[1]. But, as Renan rightly remarks, there is absolutely nothing to lead us to suppose that these "valiant heretics" were acquainted with the teachings of the Calabrian seer[2]. It is most likely that they got the doctrine (as Hugo of St Victor probably did)[3] from Erigena. It is found in his *Commentary on St John's Gospel*[4], where he teaches that there are three mystical *sacerdotia*, the first of the Old Covenant, the second of the New Covenant, reaching from John the Baptist to the end of the world, and the third of the future life.

We know scarcely anything about the life of David of Dinant. It is still doubtful whether his birthplace was Dinant on the Meuse or Dinan in Brittany. He wrote a work entitled *Quaternuli*, which was condemned and burnt at the Synod of Paris in 1209[5]. It appears to be the same[6] as that mentioned under another title, *De Tomis*, by Albert the Great[7]. David seems to have died, like Amalric, before the condemnation at Paris.

The little that we know of his teaching all seems to show that it was a reckless development of Erigena's doctrine. He appears to have shown much less regard for ecclesiastical

---

[1] Hagenbach, *History of Doctrines*, I. p. 75. R. M. Jones, *Studies in Mystical Religion*, pp. 180–7. The general notion of the "three dispensations" is, of course, as old as the Montanists.

[2] Renan, *Studies in Religious History*, pp. 214–215.

[3] Hagenbach, *History of Doctrines*, I. p. 518. Gebhart, *L'Italie mystique*, pp. 61–62.

[4] *Com. in Ev. Joh.* 308 B–309 B. (Cf. Augustine, *De Trin.* IV. 4.)

[5] Gieseler, *Ecclesiastical History*, III. p. 297.

[6] M. de Wulf, *Histoire de la philosophie médiévale*, p. 249.

[7] *Summa Theol.* Pt. I. tract. IV. qu. 20, mem. 2.

doctrine than Amalric and to have taught a frank Pantheism[1]. We can easily believe that such teaching, in such an age, may have resulted in the Antinomianism[2] that was charged upon his followers. The charges of immorality were not made in 1209, and appear to have been made later only against the followers of David, and not against the Amalricians.

That David's doctrine was grossly Pantheistic, and that it should be therefore sharply distinguished from that of Amalric, appears from the account of it given by Thomas Aquinas. He says that David divided all existing things into three classes—bodies, souls, and eternal substances. The first and indivisible element which constitutes bodies is called matter (*Hyle*, ὕλη); the first and indivisible element which constitutes souls is called intelligence (*Noys*, νοῦς); the first and indivisible element which constitutes eternal substances is called God; and these three primaries are one and the same, whence it follows that all things in the universe are essentially one[3].

---

[1] Le caractère particulier de David, c'est, comme on l'a vu, d'être un philosophe qui semble ignorer tous les dogmes, tous les mystères de l'orthodoxie chrétienne. Amaury de Chartres est, au contraire, un théologien qui prétend démontrer que le panthéisme est la vraie doctrine de saint Paul et de tous les Pères à qui la foi des simples n'a pas suffi. Hauréau, *Histoire de la philosophie scolastique*, II. (i), p. 86.

[2] *Si aliquis est in Spiritu Sancto, aiebant, et faciat fornicationem, aut aliqua alia pollutione polluatur: non est ei peccatum, quia ille Spiritus, qui est Deus, omnino separatus a carne, non potest peccare: quamdiu ille Spiritus, qui est Deus, est in eo, ille operatur omnia in omnibus.* Caesarius of Heisterbach, *De Miraculis*, v. 22. See Hagenbach, *History of Doctrines*, I. p. 484.

[3] *Quomodam antiquorum philosophorum error fuit, quod Deus esset de essentia omnium rerum. Ponebant enim, omnia esse unum simpliciter, et non differre, nisi forte secundum sensum vel aestimationem, ut Parmenides dicit; et illos etiam antiquos philosophos secuti sunt quidam moderni, ut David de Dinando. Divisit enim res in partes tres, in corpora, animas, et substantias aeternas*

Elsewhere Thomas Aquinas expressly distinguishes between the errors of Amalric and of David. He enumerates three errors with regard to the being of God, and goes on to say that while Amalric taught that God is the *principium formale*, the third error is that of David, who most foolishly taught that the *materia prima* is God[1].

Albert the Great, from whom Thomas Aquinas derived his knowledge of David, has a similar statement of his doctrine. Matter, intelligence, and God are the three primaries from which all material, intelligent and spiritual existence is constituted. As primary and indivisible, these principles are simplex, and therefore incapable of differences. Consequently they are the same, and all existence is one. The appearance of distinction and difference is an illusion of the senses[2].

---

separatas. Et primum indivisibile, ex quo constituuntur corpora, dixit ὕλη, h. e. materiam. Primum autem indivisibile, ex quo constituuntur animae, dixit νοῦς, h. e. mentem. Primum autem indivisibile in substantiis aeternis dixit Deum: et haec tria esse unum et idem. Thomas Aquinas, *Sentent.* lib. II. dist. 17, qu. 1, art. 1. See Hagenbach, *History of Doctrines,* I. p. 484.

[1] *Alii autem dixerunt, Deum esse principium formale omnium rerum, et haec dicitur fuisse opinio Almaricianorum. Tertius error fuit Davidis de Dinando, qui stultissime posuit, Deum esse materiam primam. Summa Theol.* Pt. I. qu. 3, art. 8.

[2] *Sunt quidam haeretici dicentes, Deum et materiam primam et noun sive mentem idem esse. Quod sic probant: Quaecunque sunt, et nullam differentiam habent, eadem sunt. Idem enim est, ut dicit Aristoteles* VII *topicorum, quod non differt differentia. Deus, nous, et materia prima sunt, et nullam differentiam habent: ergo eadem sunt. Quod autem haec tria sint et plura principia rerum, ex hoc volebant probare, quod res sint triplices, scilicet materiales, spirituales et divinae, nec ex uno principio proprio formabiles. Primum ergo principium formationis materialium est materia, ut dicunt; et primum principium formationis spiritualium, in quibus principium vitae est, dicunt, quod est nous sive mens. Dicunt enim, quod omnia, quae sunt in uno genere, ex uno aliquo principio simplici formantur, ut patet in omnibus generibus entis, scilicet substantia, quantitate, qualitate, et sic de aliis. Similiter divinum esse multiplex est, ut*

David of Dinant, in fact, taught a materialistic Pantheism. The first and final substance, the principle of all existence, is matter, which, conceived as the source of all intelligence, may be called intelligence, and conceived as absolute actuality, may be called God[1].

One question is inevitably suggested by the mention of Thomas Aquinas. Why did the Church condemn Erigena's teaching in such an unqualified fashion, while it accepted the later scholasticism, as represented by Aquinas, and made it the standard of Catholic philosophical doctrine to this day? There is, after all, a considerable community of thought between what has been called the earlier Latin scholastic represented by Erigena[2], and the later scholastic which reached its climax in Aquinas. They share, to a large extent, the same Neoplatonist doctrine of God, and of evil—which are the two poles of any religious philosophy. A hundred different coincidences in thought upon other matters might easily be pointed out. Yet the later scholastic philosophy of Aquinas is the very standard of orthodoxy, while the

dicunt, et necesse est, quod ex aliquo uno formetur principio, et hoc dicunt esse Deum. Haec ergo tria sunt simplicia prima: et si sunt simplicia, nullam differentiam habent: quaecunque enim habent differentias, sunt composita. Et sic suam volunt probasse intentionem. Et in hoc errore fuit David de Dinanto. Summa Theol. Pt. I. tract. 6, qu. 29, mem. I, art. 2. See Gieseler, Ecclesiastical History, III. p. 298.

[1] Tout être, selon David, est à la fois matière, esprit, et Dieu. Ces trois termes désignent, d'après lui, trois substances simples et par conséquent iden-tiques, car il n'existe qu'une substance simple....La substance première de David de Dinant n'est donc autre que la matière, envisagée, à la manière de Spinoza, comme le principe de toutes les existences tant corporelles que spirituelles. La matière est Dieu en tant qu'elle est l'absolue virtualité dans le sens d'Aristote: elle est intelligence en tant qu'elle donne naissance aux types universels tels que Platon les a définis. Jundt, Histoire du panthéisme populaire au moyen âge, pp. 16–17.

[2] Duhem, Le Système du Monde, V. p. 473.

earlier scholastic philosophy of Erigena has always been under the ban of heresy.

The answer to the question is interesting and important, for it affects the whole history of philosophic thought in the Middle Ages. Perhaps the most important change that passed over mediaeval thought was that which supplemented Augustinian Neoplatonism with a qualified Aristotelianism as the basis of Latin theology. That change involved several modifications of direction and emphasis. It meant a fresh adjustment of the claims of faith and reason, a new stress upon the transcendence of God, and a new interest in the material universe which became the precursor of modern science[1]. A distinguished Italian philosopher has spoken of the two great currents in mediaeval thought as the *platonico mistico patristico* and the *peripatetico razionalistico scolastico*[2]. The terms might be criticised, but they are at least fairly descriptive of two very real and very distinct tendencies. The former might be characterised generally as the Augustinian tradition. It held the field more or less until, in the thirteenth century, Aristotle had been translated, studied and commented upon by the Dominicans[3]. It was, in fact, the influence of Aristotle upon Aquinas that modified profoundly the whole conception of the relation of the world, and of the relation of man, to God. Speaking broadly, the result was a greatly increased emphasis upon the reality of the material universe. Theologically it meant a larger stress upon the transcendence of God, and hence a retreat from the direction of Pantheism[4].

[1] Cf. E. Gilson, *La Philosophie au Moyen Age*, I. p. 122.
[2] Cf. Rotta, *Il Pensiero di Nicolò da Cusa*, p. 90.
[3] E. Gilson, *Le Thomisme*, pp. 17–20.
[4] *Ibid.* p. 77.

In his doctrine of man, Aquinas considerably modifies the Augustinian conception. He links the exercise of reason, even in the search for the vision of God, with the faculties which are seated in the body[1]: the bond between the physical and the psychical is much closer than in a thinker like Erigena, where the sole function of the mental powers, in their association with the body, is the accumulation and assortment of sense impressions. There is a similar tendency, on the larger scale, in Aquinas' theory of the universe. The sensible world is definitely interposed between the soul and God: it is not merely, as in Erigena, a projection, first, of the mind of God, *causaliter*, and second, of the mind of man, *effectualiter*, but it possesses a more definite and, so to speak, a more independent actuality.

It is difficult to make the contrast clear by definite citations from Erigena, because he guards himself, by saving clauses, from what seems to be the logical tendency of his doctrine. For example, he says quite definitely that God is not the genus of the creature, nor the creature a species of God[2], and yet the whole drift of his system is to place God at the apex of being, and to show that all existence emanates in stages from that *summum genus* and returns by stages to it. It is true, again, that he persistently speaks of God as superessential, and therefore of His being as logically equivalent to non-being, but the whole impression remains of the graded existence of the universe reaching up to its highest grade in the superexistence of God. On the other hand, the great principle which Aquinas learned from Aristotle, and which he could scarcely have learned elsewhere,

[1] M. de Wulf, *Introduction à la philosophie néo-scolastique*, XVI. 82. E. Gilson, *Le Thomisme*, pp. 143, 149–150.
[2] *De Div. Nat.* 523 D.

was "the principle that 'being is predicated equivocally,' or, in other words, that the categories form an irreducible plurality[1]." That was a lesson of the first importance—to regard the fundamental modes of being as irreducible and not as species of a *summum genus*. Indeed, with Aquinas being is not itself a genus[2]. And the sense in which God is present in the creation is not that of an ultimate essence, giving reality to that in which it resides, but that of an agent present in that in which it acts. God is not the essence of all; He is the cause of all and the exemplar of all[3].

There is another marked difference between Erigena and the Angelic Doctor which influences this particular point. It is the doctrine of the Scot that the real being of the universe derives from God, but that all the difference and division in the world are due to evil. (There is some ambiguity upon the point, as has been pointed out elsewhere, but this is certainly the main drift of Erigena's doctrine.)

The passage from unity into multiplicity is regarded as in a measure a lapse from the reality of being, which is equated with goodness. Anything is more good and more real as it approaches the one and the indivisible. But Aquinas definitely teaches that the multiplicity and divisions of the world are directly the work of the Creator, and are not to be regarded as implying imperfection[4]. This, once more, discounts the conception which, representing much of actual existence as either illusory, or as the result of evil, leaves only a core of essential being to be regarded as directly derived from God. It is plain that the doctrine of

---

[1] A. E. Taylor, *St Thomas as a Philosopher*, pp. 27–28.
[2] *Summa Theol.* Pt. I. qu. 3, art. 5.
[3] *Ibid.* Pt. I. qu. 3, art. 8, ad. 1, Pt. I. qu. 8, art. 1.
[4] *Ibid.* Pt. I. qu. 47, art. 1.

Aquinas here both emphasises the reality of the material world as it is, and at the same time makes it less of an emanation from the essence of God, and more of an act of His will.

There is still another important point of divergence between Erigena and Aquinas which bears upon this issue. In Erigena the act, or rather the process of creation, is regarded as necessary; it is grounded in the essence of God, for goodness is creative in its very nature. (It is true that here, again, Erigena guards himself, and seeks to show that the necessity is a moral and therefore a free necessity.) But in Aquinas it is quite definitely taught that there is no such necessity[1]. The creation is the result of an act of the will of God, and (though His will is identified with His essence) that act of will might not have taken place[2]. Now it is obvious that this, again, makes the link between God and

---

[1] Der Zweck des göttlichen Willens, durch den die Dinge im Sein geschaffen worden sind, ist die göttliche Güte selber, die auch ohne die Geschöpfe absolut vollkommen wäre. Folglich ist der Zweck des göttlichen Willens absolut nicht bedingt durch das Dasein der Geschöpfe, und die Finalursache der Geschöpfe bringt keine Notwendigkeit des Daseins der letzteren mit sich. Es ist also in keiner Weise notwendig, dass die Geschöpfe existieren, und folglich kann man auch nicht behaupten, dass sie ewig sein müssen. Dr P. A. Rohner, *Das Schöpfungsproblem bei Thomas von Aquin*, p. 127.

La création est un acte éminemment libre. Elle n'est nécessitée ni par la nature de Dieu, ni par les lois de son intelligence, ni même absolument par sa justice. C. Jourdain, *La Philosophie de S. Thomas d'Aquin*, 1. p. 229.

La création n'introduit en Dieu aucune relation à l'égard de la créature; ici encore la relation est unilatérale et elle s'établit seulement entre la créature et le créateur comme entre l'être et son principe. Nous devons donc nous tenir firmement à cette conclusion que Dieu se veut et ne veut nécessairement que soi-même; que si la surabondance de son être et de son amour le porte à se vouloir et à s'aimer jusque dans les participations finies de son être, il ne faut voir là qu'un don gratuit, rien qui ressemble, même de loin, à une nécessité. E. Gilson, *Le Thomisme*, p. 103.

[2] *Summa Theol.* Pt. I. qu. 19, art. 3, and qu. 25, art. 6, ad. 3.

the world less organic, and emphasises the separation, where Erigena rather emphasises the connexion, between the Creator and the creation. There can be very little doubt that it was at points like these that the Church felt that Erigena was essentially Pantheistic, and that Aquinas was essentially Theistic.

With respect to the great philosophical controversy of the later Middle Ages, Erigena occupies a peculiar position. He has been claimed both as the first Realist, and as the first Nominalist. This is not so paradoxical as it looks.

For, on the one hand, there is no doubt that Erigena's doctrine is Realism, in the mediaeval sense of the term. The universal is the most real, for it is earlier than the individual. The divine dialectic ranges the universal first, and then descends to the particular, which is nothing more than a differentiation of the universal[1]. The universal is therefore logically and ideally prior to the particular, and the cause of it. And not only logically and ideally, for Erigena's doctrine that everything exists more truly in the knowledge of that which is above it than it exists in itself means that there is a scale of reality in which the universal is more real than the particular, the ideal more real than the phenomenal. In short, as has been well said, "so uncompromising a Platonist as the Scot could not but be a realist in his ontology[2]."

Yet, on the other hand, there is some slight historical and philosophical justification for reckoning Erigena as, in a remote sense, the first of the Nominalists. The usual view has been that Roscelin and Anselm were the protagonists

---

[1] Huber, *Johannes Scotus Erigena*, p. 238.

[2] R. L. Poole, *Illustrations of the History of Medieval Thought*, p. 99.

Dans la question des universaux, Scot est le plus exagéré des réalistes. M. de Wulf, *Histoire de la philosophie médiévale*, p. 196.

on either side of the great dispute. But in a chronicle of the tenth century[1], known only in a citation, Robert of Paris, Roscelin of Compiègne, and Arnulf of Laon are mentioned as being, in the art of dialectic, followers of John the Sophist, *qui eandem artem sophisticam vocalem esse disseruit.* There is something to be said for the identification of this John the Sophist with Erigena[2].

There seems to be a Nominalist tendency in Heric of Auxerre, and more distinctly in Berengar of Tours, both of whom were largely influenced by Erigena[3]. It is conceivable that this may be the result of suggestions in Erigena's work. He had said, for example, that dialectic was "the searcher out of the common conceptions of the mind[4]." It has been remarked that "it was easy to carry this train of reasoning a stage further, and to argue that the general terms with which logic occupies itself are not its source but its product. The universals, the Scot had agreed, are words; what if they be mere words[5]?"

[1] *Historia a Roberto Rege ad Mortem Philippi I,* in Du Boulay, *Hist. Univ. Paris,* II. p. 443.

[2] Wohl hingegen zeigt sich uns jene principielle Anschauung, wornach man wie gesagt, mit richtigen Instincte den Nominalismus in eine Verbindung mit der Lehre des Scotus Erigena brachte, in jener Stelle eines Chronisten, welche seit Bulaeus oft genug angeführt, aber nicht immer richtig verstanden wurde. Prantl, *Geschichte d. Logik im Abendlande,* II. pp. 76–77. See also Hauréau, *Histoire de la philosophie scolastique,* I. p. 244; R. L. Poole, *Illustrations of the History of Medieval Thought,* pp. 99–100. Mr R. L. Poole, in his article on Erigena in the *Dictionary of National Biography,* describes this identification as "hazardous." In his *Illustrations of the History of Medieval Thought,* which is twenty-five years earlier in date, he had thought it probable, in the light of Prantl's arguments. No man writes with greater authority on a point like this, and Mr Poole's later opinion must carry great weight.

[3] Rashdall, *Universities of Europe in the Middle Ages,* I. p. 46.

[4] *De Div. Nat.* 475 A. Erigena's words are: *communium animi conceptionum rationabilium diligens investigatrixque disciplina.*

[5] R. L. Poole, *Illustrations of the History of Medieval Thought,* pp. 99–100.

There was a double strain in Erigena's logical theory, and while he was a Realist of the Realists, some of his successors may have developed an early Nominalism, or rather Conceptualism, from one side of his teaching. For the fact is that Erigena's doctrine, on the point at issue, is a blending of the most characteristic notions of Plato and Aristotle. He "does not separate his Platonic theory of ideas as pre-existent exemplars from the Aristotelian doctrine of the universal as *in* the individuals." It would even be true to say that he deliberately and insistently combines the two. For, as Ueberweg goes on to point out, his theory is really a result of the union of the Aristotelian "Substance" with the Platonic "Idea," and of the identification of the relation of accidents to the Substance in which they inhere with that of the individuals to the idea of which they are copies[1].

Coming down to later times, the influence of Erigena is distinctly traceable along two lines—through Eckhart and the German mystics, and through Nicholas of Cusa and some of the Renaissance philosophies. There are also, of course, cross connections between these schools of thought.

There has been a disposition on the part of the few English writers who have touched upon the subject, while admitting the remarkable parallels that exist between Erigena and many mystics and philosophers of later times, to deny the

[1] Ueberweg, *History of Philosophy*, I. p. 363.

Ergibt sich uns aber schon aus dem Bisherigen als Resultat das anscheinend Widerspruchsvolle, das Scotus, der Platoniker und Anhänger des Pseudo-Dionysius, zugleich die Veranlassung zum Hervortreten einer nominalischen Partei darbieten konnte, so schienen die Belege für diese eigenthümliche Thatsache auch noch anderweitig sich zu vermehren. Was nemlich die nähere Darlegung der Aufgabe der Dialektik bei Scotus betrifft, so finden wir allerdings zunächst durchgängig den platonischen Doppelweg verquickt mit dem Schul-Mechanismus der *Tabula logica* des Porphyrius oder Boethius. Prantl, *Geschichte der Logik in Abendlande*, II. p. 27.

very possibility of any real transmission of ideas. Thus, a very competent writer, after noting a point of resemblance between Erigena and Giordano Bruno, remarks that the latter "of course cannot have read his mediaeval precursor[1]." But it is at least certain that Bruno knew the whole substance of Erigena's doctrine through Nicholas of Cusa, of whom he was a declared follower, as Nicholas in turn was a professed disciple of the Scot. Again, the ablest of all the English writers who have dealt with Erigena remarks that he "added to philosophy not a few of the salient ideas which we connect with the modern school of metaphysics. His own views were doubtless buried with his writings: they were found out afresh by other men before their publication proved how they had been anticipated[2]." This is surely a somewhat unwarrantable conclusion[3]. The appearance of the heresy of Amalric of Bena and David of Dinant, three hundred and fifty years after Erigena's death, and the hue and cry after the Scot's writings which immediately began, are alone enough to show that his views were by no means "buried with his writings." And, as has been said, there is reason to suppose that Erigena's teaching was active among many of the mystical sects of the later Middle Ages. It is admitted that thirteenth and fourteenth century mysticism derived largely from the pseudo-Dionysius, through Erigena's Latin version, and there is a growing certainty that it derived also from Erigena's own writings. The Papal ban cannot have been universally effective, for at all the strategic points in

[1] Thomas Whittaker, *Apollonius of Tyana and other Essays*, p. 128.

[2] R. L. Poole, *Illustrations of the History of Medieval Thought*, p. 73.

[3] Bien que la philosophie de Jean Scot semble avoir été incomprise de ses contemporains, elle exerça sur le développement de la pensée du moyen âge occidental une influence considérable, dont on poursuit l'action jusqu'au XIIIe siècle. M. de Wulf, *Histoire de la philosophie médiévale*, p. 198.

the suggested line of influence we definitely know that Erigena's work was accessible, and was actually studied to good purpose[1].

An independent and impartial study of the field leads to the deliberate conclusion that Erigena's influence upon mediaeval mysticism, and upon the later philosophies, is much more considerable than has been generally allowed[2].

In any case it is certain that Eckhart, the father of all the German mystics, was well acquainted with the doctrines of the Scot. When he "left Paris for his great career as a preacher in Strasbourg, he certainly carried away with him

[1] Erigena's great work is found in two catalogues of monastic libraries of the fourteenth and fifteenth centuries. Manitius, *Geschichte d. lat. Literatur d. Mittelalters*, p. 329. Writing of an earlier period, a Catholic authority (M. Jaquin, in a paper on *L'influence doctrinale de Jean Scot au début du XIIIe siècle*, in *Revue des Sciences philosophiques et théologiques*, 1907, pp. 104-6) thinks it possible that the Cistercian abbeys were exempted by the Pope from the ban on Erigena's writings. It is a striking fact that Isaac de Stella, Garnier de Rochefort, and Alain de Lille, who were all influenced by Erigena's doctrine, were all Cistercians.

[2] It is refreshing to find that two considerable foreign authorities are in agreement with the independent conclusion stated above. After commenting upon the relation between the doctrine of Erigena and that of Gilbert de la Porrée, Kaulich says: "Neben Gilberts Schriften weist der im zwölften Jahrhunderte sich gelten machende Mysticismus, wenn er überhaupt noch eine wissenschaftliche Basis besitzt, gewiss nur auf Erigena zurück; denn aus dem Nominalismus, wie überhaupt aus der Richtung des Denkens, welche die Grundlehren der peripatetischen Schule zu den ihrigen machte, dürfte das Entstehen des Mysticismus schwerlich begreiflich gemacht werden können." *Entwicklung der scholastischen Philosophie von Johannes Scotus Erigena bis Abälard*, p. 24. And M. François Picavet says: "Enfin on sait que les mystiques comme Eckhart et Jacob Boehme sont les véritables ancêtres des grands philosophes de l'Allemagne moderne, de Kant et de Fichte, d'Hegel et de Schelling, de Baader et de Schopenhauer. On sait aussi que les mystiques sont les vrais successeurs de Jean Scot et que si tous ne l'ont pas lu ou médité, tous s'en sont inspirés par des intermédiaires plus ou moins nombreux, mais dont on connaît les noms et les œuvres." *Esquisse d'une Histoire générale et comparée des Philosophies médiévales*, p. 150.

as a part of himself the mystical world-view of Dionysius and Erigena[1]." It was only seventy years or so after the stir made by Amalric of Bena that the young Dominican was at the University of Paris. There can be no question as to the reality of Erigena's influence upon Eckhart's thought. The slightest summary of the great mystic's teaching will make it clear.

Thus Eckhart taught that God is above good, since He is above all opposites and all limits: He is a Nameless Nothing. He brings forth in His Son the creative ideas, the archetypal forms, which are the "natured Nature," and which, when projected into space and time, are the world of creatures. Time and space are created with the world. Creation is the eternal process of God's thought. The real world is the world of archetypal ideas, and that is not created, it eternally *is*. All things are created in man, and all men are restored in Christ to that unity which they had in God before Adam fell. Christ is born in the believing soul. Evil is negative; it is the privation of the good that ought to be. The redeemed spirit is finally lost in God, and yet not lost, for though it sinks into the essence of God, it can never reach the ground, and hence always knows that it is a creature[2].

All these are thoughts that Eckhart unquestionably found in Erigena, and many of them he could scarcely have found elsewhere, in the literature to which he had access.

Through Eckhart many of these characteristic doctrines filtered down into the great fourteenth century mystics who followed him—Tauler, Ruysbroeck, and the rest.

[1] Rufus M. Jones, *Studies in Mystical Religion*, p. 221. W. R. Inge, *Christian Mysticism*, p. 149.
[2] See Rufus M. Jones, *Studies in Mystical Religion*, pp. 223–241. Ullmann, *Reformers before the Reformation*, II. pp. 23–31.

It is equally certain both that Nicholas of Cusa was profoundly influenced by Eckhart, and that he was a direct disciple of Erigena[1]. He refers to Erigena more than once (under the name of Scotigena) and to his book περὶ φύσεως[2]. He classes him with Dionysius, Maximus, and Hugo of St Victor, and he quotes many of the Scot's exact phrases[3].

Nicholas is one of the most astonishing figures of the fifteenth century. He rose rapidly in the Church; was a prominent figure at the Council of Basle; went on a mission to Constantinople to bring about the union of the Eastern and Western Churches; and became Bishop of Brixen and a Cardinal.

The philosophy of Nicholas is set forth in his principal work, *De docta ignorantia*, which appeared in 1440. There is a striking parallel between the whole system of the Cardinal and that of the Scot, for Nicholas begins with the superessential Unity of God, and goes on to treat the finite world as a manifestation of the Godhead—it is an apparition of the invisible, the Infinite in limitation, the Eternal in succession. He sees the Trinity reflected throughout the creation, the essence of all things being from the Father, actuality from the Son, and order from the Spirit. He teaches that all the divisions and diversity of the finite world are due to sin, and are restored to unity in Christ, and so merged into the Deity, though the individuality of things is retained. Nicholas has the Scot's complete doctrine of God as unknowable, and yet known through His works, and as the unity of oppositions, beyond all affirmation and negation,

[1] Rotta, *Il Pensiero di Nicolò da Cusa nei suoi rapporti storici*, p. 205 sqq. Rufus M. Jones, *Spiritual Reformers of the Sixteenth and Seventeenth Centuries*, p. 3.

[2] Nicolas of Cusa, *Opera*, pp. 70–73 (Basle, 1565).

[3] Erdmann, *History of Philosophy*, I. pp. 534–7.

all attributes that are distinguished in our minds being one and the same in Him. He has also Erigena's doctrine of being and non-being, the superexistent being equated with the non-existent, because both are beyond the reach of our understanding. There are many minor coincidences, and several of Erigena's favourite arguments and metaphors are closely reproduced[1] by Nicholas[2].

Giordano Bruno, again, was a professed disciple of "the divine Cusanus," as he called him[3]. It is scarcely possible that he had read Erigena for himself, but he must have known all the leading thoughts of the Scot through Nicholas. Moreover, Bruno was considerably influenced by the *Fons Vitae* of Avicebron, and repeatedly quotes the Jewish philosopher with approval[4].

There is little system in Bruno's writings, but they abound with thoughts which came from Erigena through Ibn-Gebirol and Nicholas of Cusa. Thus he teaches that God is Unity, wholly simplex, and yet the source of all number, the monad of monads (*monadum monas*), the essence of essences, the soul of souls, the nature of nature[5]. All attributes are one in Him. He is above good and evil, but our highest conception of Him is that of goodness. The Trinity is the

---

[1] See Pünjer, *History of the Christian Philosophy of Religion*, pp. 70–87. Fairbairn, *Philosophy of the Christian Religion*, pp. 102–3. P. Rotta, *Il Pensiero di Nicolò de Cusa nei suoi rapporti storici*, pp. 205 sqq.

[2] I propose in a future monograph on the philosophy of Nicholas of Cusa to deal in some detail with the connection between the teaching of Erigena, Eckhart, and Nicholas. Sufficient warrant for the statements in the text may be found, however, in the authorities quoted in the preceding notes.

[3] Dr W. Boulting, *Giordano Bruno*, p. 29.

[4] "At all events the work of the Jewish Neo-Platonist Avicebron (Ibn-Gebirol) was known to him and freely used by him." Pollock, *Spinoza*, p. 96.

[5] Dr W. Boulting, *Giordano Bruno*, pp. 138, 203, 228. J. L. McIntyre, *Giordano Bruno*, pp. 142–7.

schema of creation, and all things are a manifestation of God.

Then, again, it is acknowledged that Spinoza was considerably influenced both by Bruno and by earlier Jewish philosophy[1], especially by Maimonides, and the book *Zohar*[2]. Now we know that the *Zohar* presents some astonishing coincidences with Erigena's doctrine, and there is much reason to suppose that the Kabbalists who wrote it were familiar with the Scot's work[3]. There is therefore a definite possibility of connection, by more than one route, between the thoughts of the Scot and those of the philosopher of Amsterdam[4].

But the most startling fact about the philosophy of Erigena, in its most general aspect, is that it presents so remarkable a parallel to modern idealism, and especially to the philosophy of Hegel[5]. It is difficult to suppose, in spite of the parallels,

---

[1] "The internal evidence for Spinoza's knowledge of Bruno...is of such strength as to carry all but irresistible conviction." Pollock, *Spinoza*, p. 97.

[2] *Ibid.* p. 94.

[3] Duhem, *Le Système du Monde*, v. pp. 84, 114-115, 137, 156-7.

[4] "The pantheist or mystical element is traced to the mediaeval Jewish philosophers, with whose works we know that Spinoza was familiar. This is to some extent matter of direct evidence. A claim has been put in, and with likelihood practically amounting to certainty, for Giordano Bruno." Pollock, *Spinoza*, p. 82.

[5] It is not surprising that this should have impressed the German expositors of Erigena, Christlieb and Huber, especially as they wrote in 1860 and 1861. They characterise Erigena's scheme of thought, again and again, as "ein Vorspiel des neueren Idealismus." So Christlieb writes: Denn wenn der Grundgedanke der neuen deutschen Philosophie mit Recht darin gefunden wird, dass sie über dem Dualismus von Geist und Natur steht, sofern der Geist in ihr nicht ein Glied dieses Gegensatzes, sondern das Ganze, sein Wesen das Wesen des Wirklichen überhaupt ist, und als derjenige, welcher diesen Grundgedanken zuerst aussprach, gewöhnlich Jakob Böhme genannt wird, so können wir die Spur desselben innerhalb der anglogermanischen Völker noch um sieben Jahrhunderte zurückdatiren auf Scotus Erigena, der, sei es auch mit

that there is any real connection of thought, though it may be suggested that Hegel's knowledge of Erigena's system is perhaps greater than has been generally recognised. We know that Hegel was delighted to find vestiges of his own philosophy in the German mystics. It is not too much to say that wherever he found them, they were mainly echoes of Erigena through Eckhart. Then, apart from the indirect influence of Erigena, through Eckhart, Nicholas of Cusa, and Giordano Bruno—all of whom Hegel read sympathetically—we know that he made a careful study of Erigena's system in the work of Hjort[1].

The whole conception of dialectic as grounded in the nature of things, that the rational is the real, and the real the rational, that thought and being are essentially one; that pure Being, in its utter lack of distinction, is equivalent to Non-Being; that every higher category is the truth of the lower, all through the scale of existence, and that the Absolute Idea is the final truth of which all lower forms of thought and of being are partial expressions—all these are express doctrines of Erigena which are repeated in Hegel.

Then, within the specially Christian sphere of thought, the conception of the Trinity as the life-process of the Absolute; of the Incarnation as the manifestation in time of the spiritual nature of man as eternally grounded in God; of the Logos as the unity of the differences of the world; of the Holy Spirit as Love, the mutual bond between the

noch nicht ganz klarem Bewusstsein, es doch einmal aussprach, dass der Geist und die Natur, das Denken und sein Object in keinem Gegensatz stehen, dass vielmehr das letztere seine Substanz nur im ersteren habe, dass der intellectus die erkannte Sache selbst sei. *Leben u. Lehre d. Johannes Scotus Erigena*, p. 291.

[1] P. Hjort, *Johannes Scotus Erigena, oder von dem Ursprung einer christlichen Philosophie*, 1823.

diverse unity of the nature of God; of creation as a process rather than an act, a necessary process resulting from the very nature of God, a series of moments in the life of God; and hence of the distinction between the absolute reality of the eternal world, and the merely phenomenal reality of the world of time and space and sense—all these are equally distinct and equally characteristic doctrines of Hegel and of his mediaeval forerunner.

Whatever may be thought as to the actual transmission of the Scot's thoughts, along these suggested lines of contact, there can at least be no doubt that he had the rare distinction of being the precursor, by several centuries, of the most profound mysticism of the later Middle Ages, and of the most daring philosophies of modern times[1].

[1] Hauréau, *Histoire de la philosophie scolastique*, I. p. 151.

APPENDIX

THE SCRIPTURAL QUOTATIONS IN THE WRITINGS OF ERIGENA

I have examined and identified all Erigena's quotations from Scripture. Every case in which he varies from the text of the Vulgate is dealt with in the following notes:

Gen. i. 2.

In 548 A gives *invisibilis et incomposita* as the equivalent of the LXX (ἀόρατος καὶ ἀκατασκεύαστος, but does not quote the Greek). Erigena found *invisibilis et incomposita* given as the translation of the LXX in Rufinus' version of Origen (*De Princ.* IV. 1). It was also the rendering found in the Old-Latin text used by Augustine (*Conf.* XII. 4 *et sqq.*). In 555 C quotes Basil for *fovebat* instead of *ferebatur*, as the equivalent of the Syriac.

Gen. i. 21.

In 742 A quotes the LXX: τὰ κήτη.

Gen. iii. 7.

In 583 C quotes the LXX: περιζώματα.

Job xl. 14.

In 418 C reads: *Hoc est initium figmenti Domini, quod fecit, ut illudatur ab angelis ejus.* (The passage is Job xl. 19 in the English versions.) Cf. LXX of the text, and LXX and Vulgate of Ps. civ. 26. In 927 C quotes a passage from Augustine (*Exem. II*) containing this rendering of the text. Augustine also quotes it in *De Civ. Dei*, XI. 15.

Ps. xl. 6.

In 1007 B reads: *corpus* for *aures* (LXX σῶμα). So Augustine, *De Civ. Dei*, XVII. 20. Also, by altering the punctuation, reads: *corpus autem perfecisti mihi holocaustum.*

Prov. viii. 22.

In 685 D reads: *creavit* for *possedit* (LXX Κύριος ἔκτισέ με). So Augustine, *Conf.* VII. 21, and *De Fide et Symbolo*, III. 6.

Isa. x. 17.

In 940 A reads: *Sanctificabo eam in igne ardente, et devorabit sicut foenum materiem.* In 960 C quotes the same rendering from Jerome (*In Expos. Ezechiel*). Cf. LXX.

Isa. xxvi. 10.

In 967 D reads: *tolletur* for *misereamur* (LXX ἀρθήτω). Cf. Augustine, *De Trin.* XIV. 19. 25.

Ezek. xvi. 53–55. In 1004 A translates the LXX.

Matt. xxiv. 35. In 887 B reads: *transibunt* for *praeteribunt*. So also in 990 A. Cf. Augustine, *De Civ. Dei*, XX. 24.

Matt. xxv. 41. In 543 B reads: *ite* for *discedite*. (So Augustine, *De Trin.* I. 13.) So also in 921 D, and *praeparatus* for *paratus*.

Luke xi. 9–10. In 602 A reads: *accipietis* for *dabitur*. So Augustine, *Conf.* XII. 1.

John i. 1. In 642 A quotes the Greek: ἐν ἀρχῇ ἦν ὁ λόγος.

John i. 3. In 559 A reads: *quod factum est in ipso, vita erat.* There is much to be said for this punctuation. It is supported by three out of five of the oldest uncials (*Codex Alexandrinus, Codex Ephraemi, Codex Bezae*) as well as by several ancient versions, such as the Old Latin (*Codex Veronensis*) and the Old Syriac, and by many of the Fathers, particularly Clement of Alexandria, Origen, and Augustine.

Rom. i. 4. In 431 A quotes the Greek: τοῦ ὁρισθέντος υἱοῦ Θεοῦ ἐν δυνάμει.

Rom. viii. 18. In 1017 B reads: *superventuram* for *futuram*.

Rom. viii. 22. In 536 B reads: *congemiscit* for *ingemiscit.*

Rom. xi. 33–36. In 1012 D reads: *inscrutabilia* for *incomprehensibilia* (so Augustine, *De Civ. Dei*, XX. 1 and *De Trin.* I. 6) and after *viae ejus* adds *in omni tempore!* (So also in 951 A.) Also, after *et in ipso*, adds *et ad ipsum.* (So also in 984 B.)

1 Cor. i. 30. In 449 B reads: *justificatio* for *justitia*.

1 Cor. xii. 8–11. In 563 C reads: *propria unicuique* for *singulis*. So Augustine, *De Trin.* XV. 19. 34.

1 Cor. xv. 51. In 979 B quotes the Vulgate as it stands: *Omnes quidem resurgemus, sed non omnes immutabimur*, but goes on to say that there are other renderings of the Apostle's words, some reading: *Omnes quidem dormiemus, sed non omnes immutabimur*, and others reading: *Omnes quidem immutabimur, sed non omnes dormiemus.* The transposition of the negative is due to the difficulty that was felt, after the Apostle's own death, in the words, "We shall not all sleep." Augustine discusses these various readings in *De Civ. Dei* XX. 20.

Ephes. i. 4. In 431 B quotes the Greek: ἐν ἀγάπῃ προορίσας ἡμᾶς.

Ephes. i. 10. In 989 D reads: *restaurari* for *instaurare*.

Ephes. iii. 11. In 431 B quotes the Greek: κατὰ πρόθεσιν Θεοῦ.

Ephes. iv. 13. In 995 C quotes the Greek: εἰς μέτρον ἡλικίας.

Phil. i. 23. In 955 C reads: *cupio* for *desiderium habens.* Cf.
Augustine, *De Civ. Dei,* XIV. 7.

Phil. iv. 7. In 446 B reads: *Christi* for *Dei* and *intellectum* for
sensum. The latter is in Augustine, *De Civ. Dei,*
XXII. 29.

Col. i. 16. In 641 B reads: *creata* for *condita* and after *per ipsum
et in ipso* adds *et ex ipso.* This addition occurs when-
ever the passage is quoted. (See Note on Romans
xi. 33–36.)

Titus ii. 11. In 371 B reads: *illuxit* for *apparuit.*

I Pet. i. 12. In 615 A reads: *concupiscunt* for *desiderant.*

The general conclusion with regard to Erigena's variations from the text of the Vulgate would seem to be that:

1. There are a few loose quotations due to lapses of
memory, as one would expect;

2. There are some instances in which he refers to the
LXX but it is possible that he had met with all these
readings (as we know he did with some of them) in the
Fathers;

3. All the remaining variants seem to be due to the
presence of quotations from the Old-Latin versions in the
Fathers, above all in Augustine.

INDEX

I. NAMES

II. SUBJECTS

III. IMPORTANT LATIN WORDS

IV. IMPORTANT GREEK WORDS